En Route:
The French
Autoroute Guide
Richard Binns

CORGI

Maps researched and drawn by the author

Les cartes ont été analysées et dessinées par l'auteur

Die Karten sind von dem Autor gezeichnet und nachgeforscht worden

Kaarten zijn getekend en onderzocht door de schrijver

A CORGI BOOK 0 552 99234 8

First publication in Great Britain

PRINTING HISTORY

Corgi edition published 1986

This book is set in Helvetica

Corgi Books are published by Transworld Publishers Ltd., 61–63 Uxbridge Road, Ealing, London W5 5SA, in Australia by Transworld Publishers (Aust.) Pty. Ltd., 26 Harley Crescent, Condell Park, NSW 2200, and in New Zealand by Transworld Publishers (N.Z.) Ltd., Cnr. Moselle and Waipareira Avenues, Henderson, Auckland.

Cover: water-colour by Denis Pannett.
Typeset by Art Photoset Limited, 64 London End, Beaconsfield, Bucks.
Printed in West Germany by Mohndruck, Gütersloh.

HOW TO USE THE GUIDE

① Study the map on pages 6 and 7. Autoroutes with sections in the guide are identified as **A6** . Each autoroute has a page number shown alongside it; this refers to the page number of the autoroute route map.

② Turn to the autoroute route map you wish to use – pages 8–22. Each route map shows autoroute exits, towns adjacent to the autoroute, service areas, rest areas and toll booths. The vast majority of exits have a number shown alongside them – printed within a square as ⟨127⟩. This is the page number of the autoroute exit map.

③ Refer to the indicated page for the specific exit information required.

④ An explanation of the symbols and abbreviations used appears on page 4.

MODE D'EMPLOI DU GUIDE

① Etudier la carte aux pages 6 et 7. Les autoroutes qui bénéficient d'une section dans le guide sont identifiées par **A6**. Chaque autoroute est accompagnée d'un numéro de page qui fait référence au numéro de la page de la carte routière des autoroutes.

② Tourner à la page de la carte routière que l'on veut utiliser – pages 8–22. Chaque carte routière montre les sorties d'autoroutes, les villes proches de l'autoroute, les aires de service et de repos, et les barrières de péage. La grande majorité des sorties sont accompagnées d'un numéro imprimé au milieu d'un carré comme ceci ⟨127⟩. Celui-ci représente le numéro de la page de la sortie d'autoroute.

③ Se reférer à la page indiquée pour obtenir l'information de sortie désirée.

④ Les explications concernant les symbôles et les abréviations utilisés se trouvent à la page 4.

GEBRAUCHSANWEISUNG DES AUTOBAHNFÜHRERS

① Studieren Sie die Karte auf Seiten 6 und 7. Die Autobahnen, für die es ein paar Seiten im Führer gibt, werden so **A6** ausgewiesen. Jede Autobahn hat eine Seitennummer. Diese Nummer weist auf die Seitennummer der Straßenkarte hin.

② Blättern Sie bis zur Straßenkarte, die Sie benutzen wollen – Seiten 8–22. Jede Straßenkarte zeigt Autobahnausfahrten, anliegende Städte, Tankstellen mit Raststätten und Mautstellen. Neben den meisten Ausfahrten steht eine Nummer – in der Mitte eines Quadrats, wie hier ⟨127⟩. Das ist die Seitennummer der Ausfahrtskarte.

③ Schlagen Sie die angegebene Seite für die bestimmte Information, die Sie brauchen auf.

④ Die Zeichen und Abkürzungen werden auf Seite 5 erklärt.

HOE DE GIDS TE GEBRUIKEN

① Bestudeer de kaarten op bladzijde 6 en 7. Autowegen met sekties in de gids zijn geindentificeerd als **A6** . Elke autoweg heeft een genummerde bladzijde er naast getoond; deze verwijst naar de genummerde bladzijde van de autoweg wegenkaart.

② Sla open op de autoweg wegenkaart die u wenst te gebruiken – bladzijde 8–22. Elke wegenkaart toont autoweg afritten, dichtsbijzijnd gelegen steden naar de autoweg, serviceplaatsen met benzinestations, rustplaatsen en tolhefkantoren. Het overgrote deel van deze afritten hebben een nummer er naast getoond – gedrukt in een vierkant, zoals ⟨127⟩. Dit is het nummer van de bladzijde van de autoweg afritten kaart.

③ Sla terug naar de aangegevan bladzijde voor de speciaal door u gewenste informatie.

④ Een uitleg van de symbolen en afkortingen die gebruikt zijn staan op bladzijde 5.

4

Route maps / Cartes routières

Symbol	English	Français
●	Autoroute exit	Sortie d'autoroute
127	Page for detailed exit map	Page de la carte de sortie détaillée
◆▮◆	Service stations (fuel)	Stations-service (essence)
◇▮◇	Rest areas	Aires de repos
♿	Facilities for disabled	Aménagements pour handicapés
✝	Toll booth	Barrière de péage

Exit maps / Cartes de sorties

20 POITIERS	Autoroute exit sign and exit number where applicable	Panneau de sortie d'autoroute et numéro de sortie s'il y en a un
⤋⤊	Autoroute exits/entries (separate arrows for each exit/entry)	Sorties d'autoroute/entrées (flèches individuelles pour chaque sortie/entrée)
✛	Toll booth	Barrière de péage
Hotels Rests	Hotels. Restaurants	Hôtels. Restaurants
(sans rest)	No restaurant	Sans restaurant
(avec ch)	With bedrooms	Avec chambres
L – LLLL	Facilities (prices vary accordingly): L simple; LL comfortable; LLL very comfortable; LLLL luxury	Caractéristiques (différents prix selon le confort): L simple; LL confortable; LLL très confortable LLLL luxueux
39100 Dole	Postal code and town name	Code postal et nom de la ville
☎	Phone number	Numéro de téléphone
F	Closed	Fermé
1 – 12	January – December	Janvier – Décembre
(Noël) (mi)	Christmas. Mid (month)	Noël. Milieu (mois)
D L Ma Me	Sunday Monday Tuesday Wednesday	Dimanche Lundi Mardi Mercredi
J V S	Thursday Friday Saturday	Jeudi Vendredi Samedi
(s) (m)	Evening. Midday	Soir. Midi
Garages	Garages	Garages
Banques	Banks	Banques
S/marché	Supermarket	Supermarché
Camping	Camping/Caravanning	Camping/Caravaning
🅿	Petrol (Gasoline) station	Station d'essence
🅥	Chemist (Doctor? Ask at chemist)	Pharmacie (Docteur? Demander à la pharmacie)
✚	Hospital	Hôpital
Pol	Police	Police/Gendarmerie
✉	Post Office	Bureau de poste
ℂ	Public telephone	Téléphone public
❶	Tourist Information Office	Office du Tourisme
🅿	Parking	Parking
⛪	Church	Eglise
✈	Airport	Aéroport
++++++	Railway	Chemin de fer
....	General shopping area	Centre commercial
→	One-way street	Voie à sens unique

Zeichenerklärung der Kartenskizzen und Abkürzungen, die in den Karten gebrauchtwerden		**Sleutel voor de symbolen en afkortingen gebruikt op de kaarten**
	Straßenkarten	**Wegenkaarten**
●	Autobahnausfahrt	Autoweg afrit
127	Seite mit detaillierter Ausfahrtskarte	Bldz. voor uitvoerige kaart voor afritten
◆❙◆	Tankstellen	Benzinestations
◇❙◇	Raststätten	Rustplaatsen
♿	Einrichtungen für Körperbehinderte	Inrichtingen voor gehandicapten
✝	Mautstelle	Tolhefkantoor
	Ausfahrtskarten	**Uitritkaarten**
20 POITIERS	Autobahnausfahrtsschild und = nummer, wenn anwendbar	Autoweg afrit teken en afrit nummer waar van toepassing
⤋	Autobahnausfahrten-einfahrten (einzelne Pfeile für jede Ausfahrt/Einfahrt)	Autoweg afritten/inritten (scheidt de pijlen voor elke afrit/inrit)
✛	Mautstelle	Tolhefkantoor
Hotels Rests	Hotels. Restaurants	Hotels. Restaurants
(sans rest)	Ohne Restaurant	Zonder restaurant
(avec ch)	Mit Zimmern	Met slaapgelegenheden
L – LLLL	Einrichtungen (Preis je nach Einrichtungen): L einfach; LL bequem; LLL sehr bequem; LLLL luxuriös	Mogelijkheden (Prijzen variëren met mogelijkheden): L eenvoudig; LL komfortabel; LLL zeer komfortabel; LLLL luxueus
39100 Dole	Postleitzahl und Stadtname	Postcode en naam van de stad
☎	Telefonnummer	Telefoon nummer
F	Geschlossen	Gesloten
1 – 12	Januar – Dezember	Januari – December
(Noël) (mi)	Weihnachten. Mitte (Monat)	Kerstmis. Midden van de maand
D L Ma Me	Sonntag Montag Dienstag Mittwoch	Zondag Maandag Dinsdag Woensdag
J V S	Donnerstag Freitag Samstag	Donderdag Vrijdag Zaterdag
(s) (m)	Abend. Mittag	Avond. Midden van de dag
Garages	Garagen	Garages
Banques	Banken	Banken
S/marché	Supermarkt	Supermarkt
Camping	Camping/Caravanning	Kampeer/Caravan plaats
🗌	Benzin. Tankstellen	Benzinestation
🗌	Apotheke (Arzt? Fragen Sie den Apotheker)	Apotheker (Dokter? Vraag apotheker)
✚	Krankenhaus	Ziekenhuis
Pol	Polizei	Politiepost
✉	Postamt	Postkantoor
☎	Öffentliche Telefonzelle	Publieke telefooncel
❶	Fremdenverkehrsamt	Touristen informatie kantoor
P	Parkplatz	Parkeerterrein
⛪	Kirche	Kerk
✈	Flughafen	Luchthaven
+++++	Eisenbahn	Spoorweg
::::::::	Einkaufszentrum	Algemeen winkel centrum
→	Einbahnstraße	Eenrichtingsverkeer

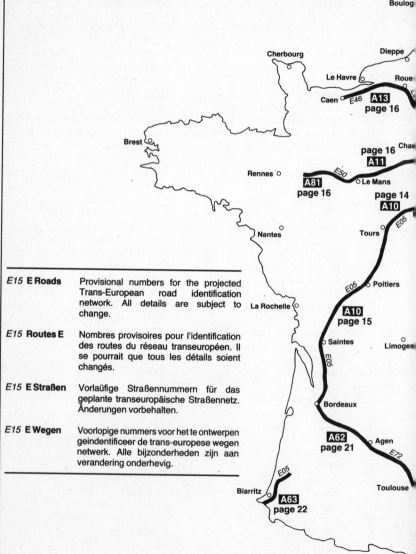

E15 **E Roads** Provisional numbers for the projected Trans-European road identification network. All details are subject to change.

E15 **Routes E** Nombres provisoires pour l'identification des routes du réseau transeuropéen. Il se pourrait que tous les détails soient changés.

E15 **E Straßen** Vorläufige Straßennummern für das geplante transeuropäische Straßennetz. Änderungen vorbehalten.

E15 **E Wegen** Voorlopige nummers voor het te ontwerpen geindentificeer de trans-europese wegen netwerk. Alle bijzonderheden zijn aan verandering onderhevig.

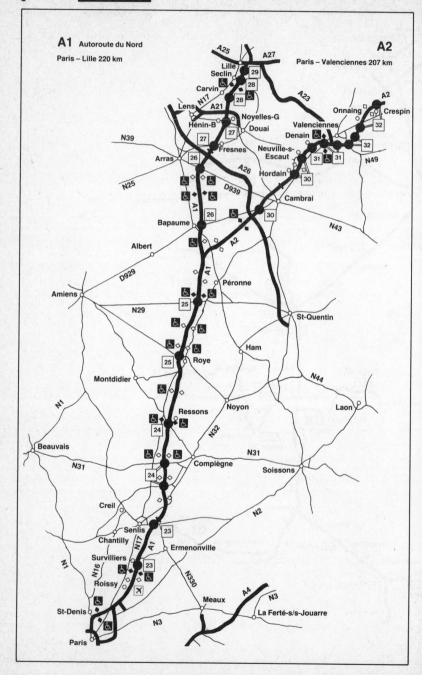

A1 Autoroute du Nord
Paris – Lille 220 km

A2
Paris – Valenciennes 207 km

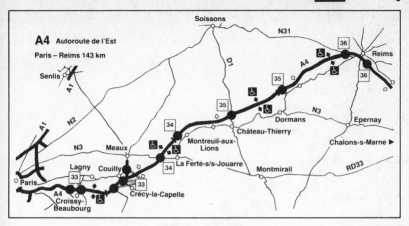

A4 Autoroute de l'Est

Paris – Reims 143 km

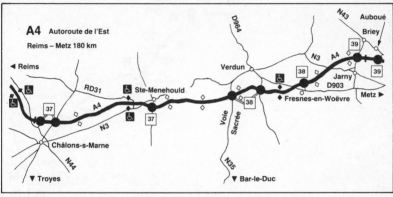

A4 Autoroute de l'Est

Reims – Metz 180 km

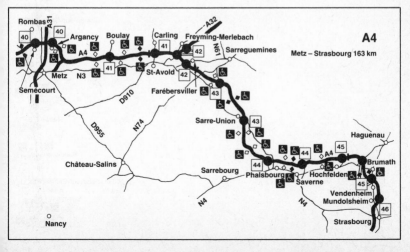

A4

Metz – Strasbourg 163 km

A6

Autoroute du Soleil **A6**

Paris – Lyon 460 km

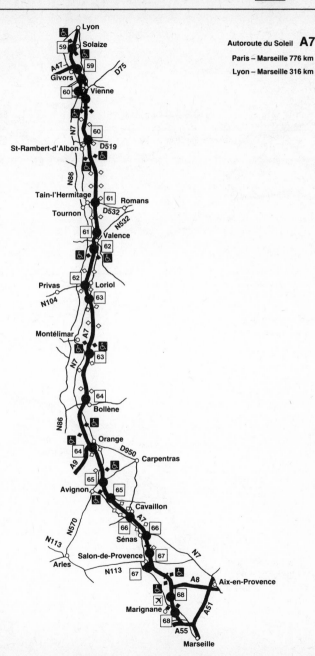

Autoroute du Soleil A7

Paris – Marseille 776 km

Lyon – Marseille 316 km

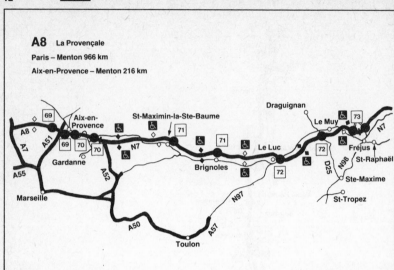

A8 La Provençale

Paris – Menton 966 km

Aix-en-Provence – Menton 216 km

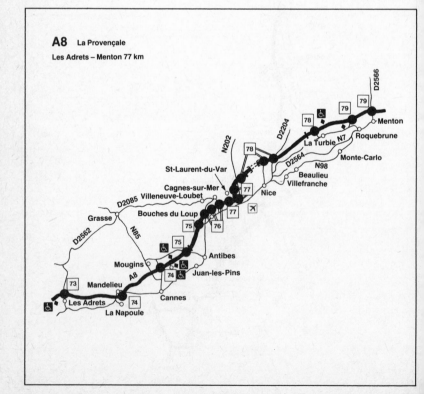

A8 La Provençale

Les Adrets – Menton 77 km

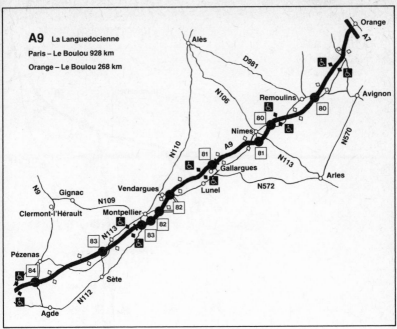

A9 La Languedocienne

Paris – Le Boulou 928 km

Orange – Le Boulou 268 km

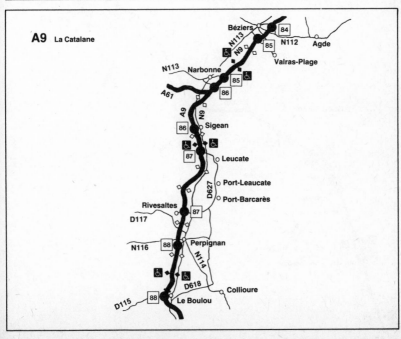

A9 La Catalane

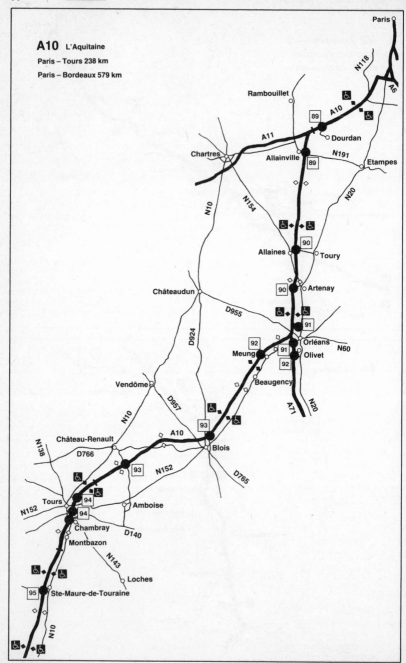

A10 L'Aquitaine

Paris – Tours 238 km

Paris – Bordeaux 579 km

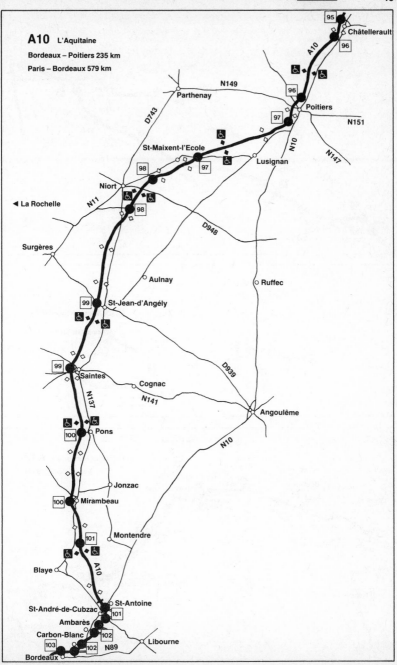

A10

15

A10 L'Aquitaine

Bordeaux – Poitiers 235 km

Paris – Bordeaux 579 km

Châtellerault

Poitiers

Parthenay

St-Maixent-l'Ecole

Lusignan

◄ La Rochelle

Niort

Surgères

Aulnay

Ruffec

St-Jean-d'Angély

Saintes

Cognac

Angoulême

Pons

Jonzac

Mirambeau

Montendre

Blaye

St-Antoine

St-André-de-Cubzac

Ambarès

Carbon-Blanc

Libourne

Bordeaux

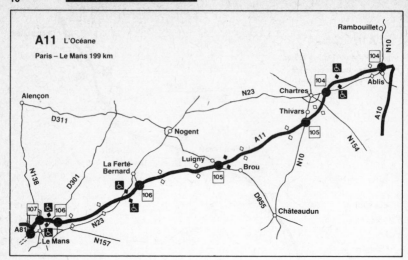

A11 L'Océane

Paris – Le Mans 199 km

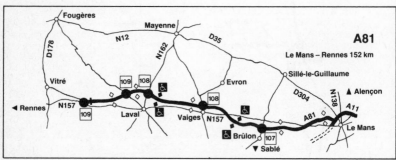

A81

Le Mans – Rennes 152 km

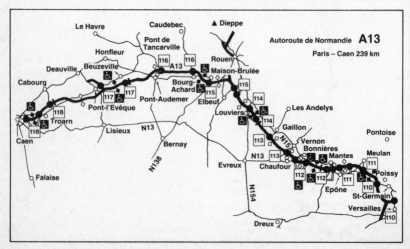

Autoroute de Normandie **A13**

Paris – Caen 239 km

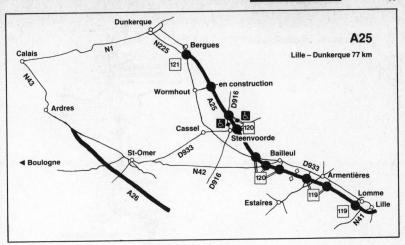

A25

Lille – Dunkerque 77 km

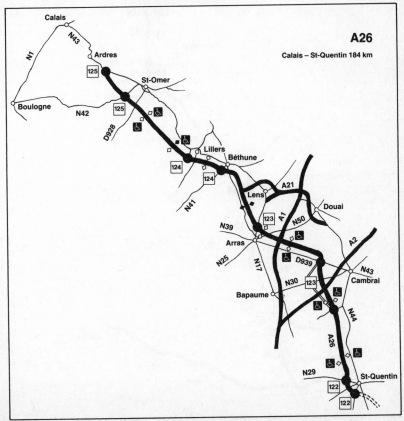

A26

Calais – St-Quentin 184 km

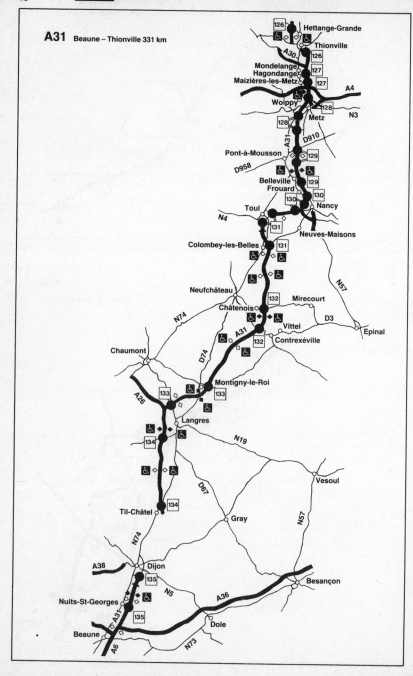

A31 Beaune – Thionville 331 km

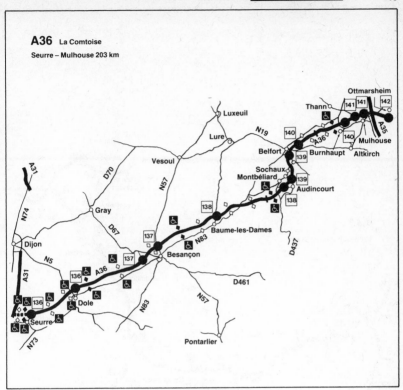

A36 La Comtoise
Seurre – Mulhouse 203 km

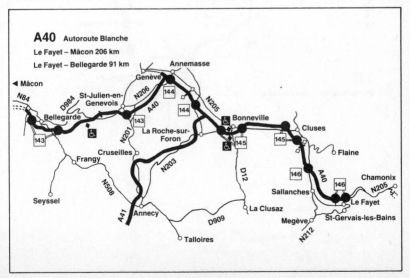

A40 Autoroute Blanche
Le Fayet – Mâcon 206 km
Le Fayet – Bellegarde 91 km

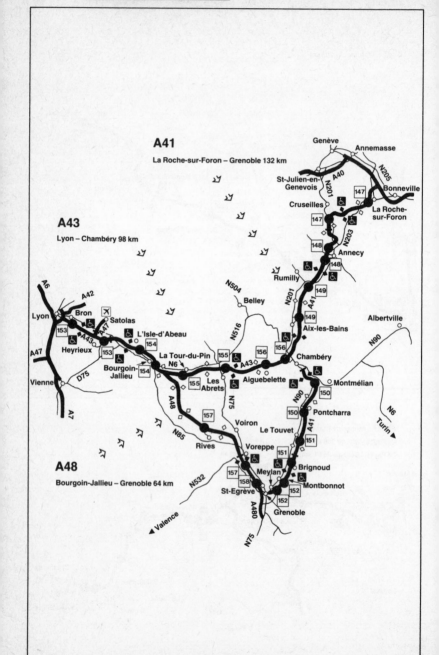

A41

La Roche-sur-Foron – Grenoble 132 km

A43

Lyon – Chambéry 98 km

A48

Bourgoin-Jallieu – Grenoble 64 km

Genève
Annemasse
N205
St-Julien-en-Genevois
A40
Bonneville
N201
147
La Roche-sur-Foron
Cruseilles
147
N203
148
Annecy
148
Rumilly
149
N504
N201
A41
Belley
149
N516
Aix-les-Bains
Albertville
156
N90
153
A42
Bron
Satolas
A6
Lyon
153
A47
L'Isle-d'Abeau
154
155
A43
Chambéry
Heyrieux
La Tour-du-Pin
156
A47
N6
150
Bourgoin-Jallieu
154
Montmélian
Vienne
D75
Les Abrets
155
Aiguebelette
N90
N6
A7
N516
150
Pontcharra
Turin
157
N75
Voiron
151
A48
A41
N85
Le Touvet
Rives
Voreppe
151
157
Meylan
Brignoud
158
152
Montbonnot
St-Egrève
152
N532
Grenoble
A480
Valence
N75

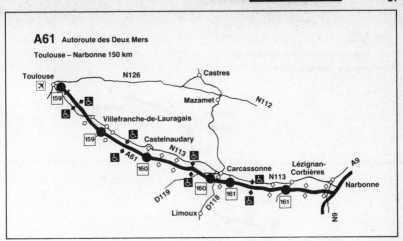

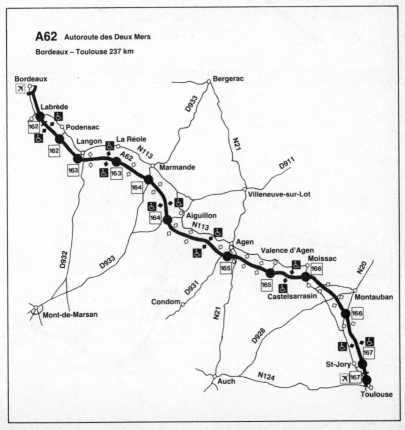

A63

St-Geours-de-Maremne – Hendaye 66 km

Bordeaux – Hendaye 214 km

N10

N124

Dax

168

A63

St-Geours-de-Maremne

St-Vincent-de-Tyrosse

Hossegor

168

D79

Capbreton

N117

Pau ▶

Bayonne

169

Biarritz

Anglet

169

St-Jean-de-Luz

170

D932

170

Cambo-les-Bains

Hendaye

N10

171

171

A72

Clermont-Ferrand – St-Etienne 146 km

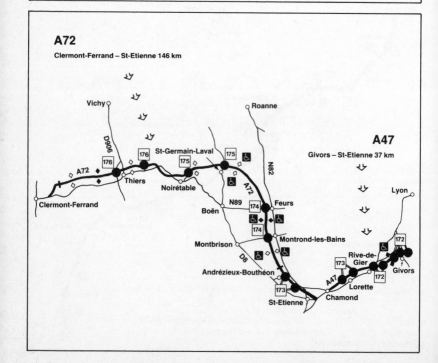

Vichy

Roanne

A47

Givors – St-Etienne 37 km

D906

176

St-Germain-Laval

175

Lyon

176

A72

175

N82

Thiers

Noirétable

A72

Clermont-Ferrand

N89

174

Feurs

Boën

174

172

Montbrison

Montrond-les-Bains

Rive-de-Gier

D8

173

172

Givors

Andrézieux-Bouthéon

A47

Lorette

173

Chamond

St-Etienne

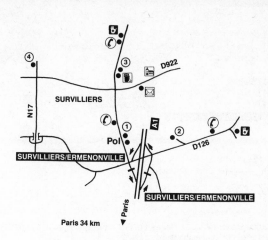

Hotels   ① **Novotel** LLL 95470 Survilliers-St-Witz ☎ (1) 34 68 69 80
       ② **Mercure** LLL 95470 Survilliers-St-Witz ☎ (1) 34 68 28 28
Garages   ③ **Garage de la Liberté** (Citroën)
S/marché ④ **Leclerc**

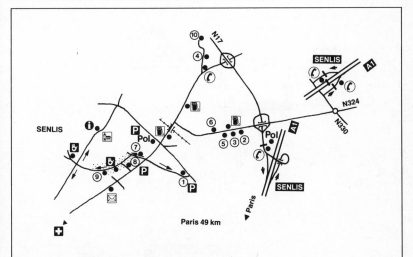

Hotels   ① **Host. de la Porte Bellon** L 60300 Senlis ☎ 44 53 03 05 F: Noël-1(mi),V
       ② **Ibis** L 60300 Senlis ☎ 44 53 70 50
       ③ **Campanile** L 60300 Senlis ☎ 44 60 05 07
Garages   ④ **Fiat** ⑤ **S.A.C.L.I** (Renault) ⑥ **Garage du Valois** (Audi/VW)
Banques   ⑦ **BNP** ⑧ **Crédit Agricole** ⑨ **Crédit Lyonnais**
S/marché ⑩ **Intermarché**

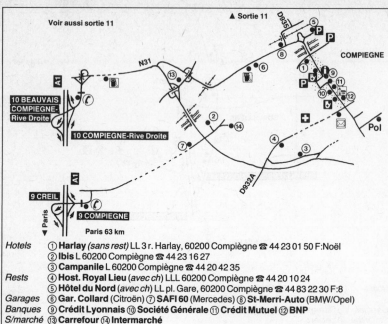

Hotels
① **Harlay** *(sans rest)* LL 3 r. Harlay, 60200 Compiègne ☎ 44 23 01 50 F:Noël
② **Ibis** L 60200 Compiègne ☎ 44 23 16 27
③ **Campanile** L 60200 Compiègne ☎ 44 20 42 35
Rests
④ **Host. Royal Lieu** *(avec ch)* LLL 60200 Compiègne ☎ 44 20 10 24
⑤ **Hôtel du Nord** *(avec ch)* LL pl. Gare, 60200 Compiègne ☎ 44 83 22 30 F:8
Garages ⑥ **Gar. Collard** (Citroën) ⑦ **SAFI 60** (Mercedes) ⑧ **St-Merri-Auto** (BMW/Opel)
Banques ⑨ **Crédit Lyonnais** ⑩ **Société Générale** ⑪ **Crédit Mutuel** ⑫ **BNP**
S/marché ⑬ **Carrefour** ⑭ **Intermarché**

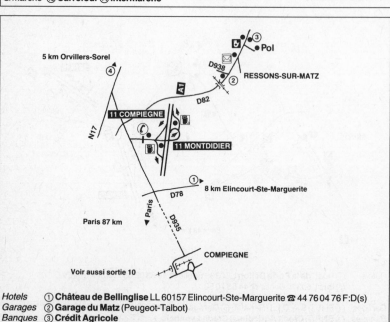

Hotels ① **Château de Bellinglise** LL 60157 Elincourt-Ste-Marguerite ☎ 44 76 04 76 F:D(s)
Garages ② **Garage du Matz** (Peugeot-Talbot)
Banques ③ **Crédit Agricole**
Camping ④ **Ch. de Sorel** Orvillers-Sorel, 60490 Ressons-sur-Matz ☎ 44 85 02 74 F:12(mi)-1

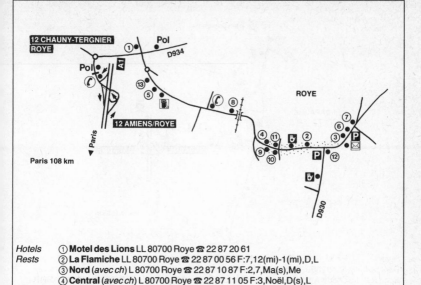

Hotels	① **Motel des Lions** LL 80700 Roye ☎ 22 87 20 61
Rests	② **La Flamiche** LL 80700 Roye ☎ 22 87 00 56 F:7,12(mi)-1(mi),D,L
	③ **Nord** (*avec ch*) L 80700 Roye ☎ 22 87 10 87 F:2,7,Ma(s),Me
	④ **Central** (*avec ch*) L 80700 Roye ☎ 22 87 11 05 F:3,Noël,D(s),L
Garages	⑤ **Roye-Autos** (Cit) ⑥ **Gar. Dallet** (Ford) ⑦ **Carlier** (PT) ⑧ **Boitel** (Audi/VW)
Banques	⑨ **Société Générale** ⑩ **Crédit Lyonnais** ⑪ **Crédit Mutuel** ⑫ **BNP**
S/marché	⑬ **Intermarché**

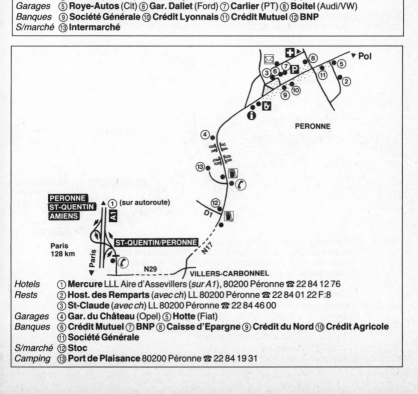

Hotels	① **Mercure** LLL Aire d'Assevillers (*sur A1*), 80200 Péronne ☎ 22 84 12 76
Rests	② **Host. des Remparts** (*avec ch*) LL 80200 Péronne ☎ 22 84 01 22 F:8
	③ **St-Claude** (*avec ch*) LL 80200 Péronne ☎ 22 84 46 00
Garages	④ **Gar. du Château** (Opel) ⑤ **Hotte** (Fiat)
Banques	⑥ **Crédit Mutuel** ⑦ **BNP** ⑧ **Caisse d'Epargne** ⑨ **Crédit du Nord** ⑩ **Crédit Agricole**
	⑪ **Société Générale**
S/marché	⑫ **Stoc**
Camping	⑬ **Port de Plaisance** 80200 Péronne ☎ 22 84 19 31

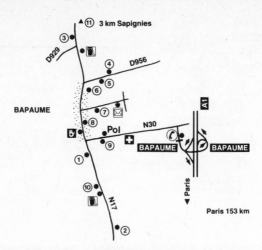

Hotels   ① **Paix** L 62450 Bapaume ☎ 21 07 11 03 F:8,Noël,S
Garages   ② **Auto 2000** (Opel) ③ **Zuliani-Roose** (Citroën)
Banques   ④ **Crédit Agricole** ⑤ **Crédit Mutuel** ⑥ **Crédit Lyonnais** ⑦ **Crédit du Nord** ⑧ **BNP**
          ⑨ **Caisse d'Epargne**
S/marché ⑩ **Intermarché**
Camping   ⑪ **Verdure** Sapignies, 62121 Achiet-le-Grand ☎ 21 07 15 47 F:12

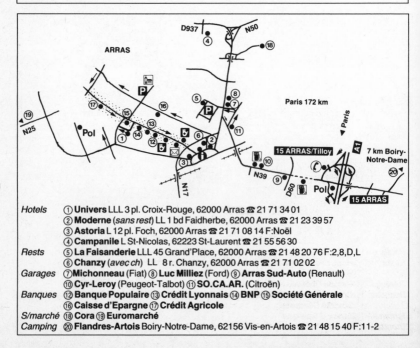

Hotels   ① **Univers** LLL 3 pl. Croix-Rouge, 62000 Arras ☎ 21 71 34 01
          ② **Moderne** (*sans rest*) LL 1 bd Faidherbe, 62000 Arras ☎ 21 23 39 57
          ③ **Astoria** L 12 pl. Foch, 62000 Arras ☎ 21 71 08 14 F:Noël
          ④ **Campanile** L St-Nicolas, 62223 St-Laurent ☎ 21 55 56 30
Rests   ⑤ **La Faisanderie** LLL 45 Grand'Place, 62000 Arras ☎ 21 48 20 76 F:2,8,D,L
          ⑥ **Chanzy** (*avec ch*) LL 8 r. Chanzy, 62000 Arras ☎ 21 71 02 02
Garages   ⑦ **Michonneau** (Fiat) ⑧ **Luc Milliez** (Ford) ⑨ **Arras Sud-Auto** (Renault)
          ⑩ **Cyr-Leroy** (Peugeot-Talbot) ⑪ **SO.CA.AR.** (Citroën)
Banques   ⑫ **Banque Populaire** ⑬ **Crédit Lyonnais** ⑭ **BNP** ⑮ **Société Générale**
          ⑯ **Caisse d'Epargne** ⑰ **Crédit Agricole**
S/marché ⑱ **Cora** ⑲ **Euromarché**
Camping   ⑳ **Flandres-Artois** Boiry-Notre-Dame, 62156 Vis-en-Artois ☎ 21 48 15 40 F:11-2

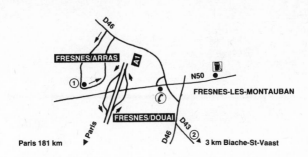

Hotels ① **Motel Grill** LLL Fresnes-lès-Montauban, 62490 Vitry-en-Artois ☎ 21 50 00 13
Camping ② **Municipal les Etangs** 62118 Biache-St-Vaast ☎ 21 50 15 02 F:11-3

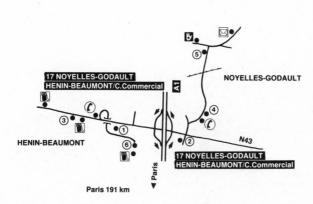

Hotels ① **Novotel** LLL Hénin-Beaumont, 62950 Noyelles-Godault ☎ 21 75 16 01
② **Campanile** L 62950 Noyelles-Godault ☎ 21 76 26 26
Garages ③ **Sandrah** (Renault) ④ **Luis de Almenera** (Ford)
Banques ⑤ **Caisse d'Epargne**
S/marché ⑥ **Auchan**

Garages ① **Deswarte** (Audi/VW) ② **Auto 3000** (Opel)
Banques ③ **Crédit Lyonnais** ④ **Société Générale** ⑤ **Crédit Agricole** ⑥ **Caisse d'Epargne**
⑦ **BNP**
S/marché ⑧ **Intermarché** ⑨ **Leclerc**

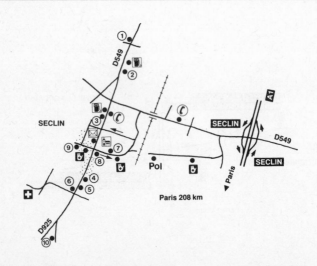

Garages ① **Philippe** (Mercedes) ② **Boutry** (Fiat) ③ **Wacrenier** (Renault) ④ **Mallet** (Audi/VW)
⑤ **Peugeot-Talbot** ⑥ **Citroën**
Banques ⑦ **Société Générale** ⑧ **Crédit Lyonnais** ⑨ **Caisse d'Epargne**
S/marché ⑩ **Champion**

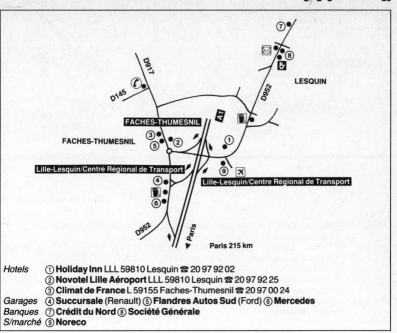

Hotels   ① **Holiday Inn** LLL 59810 Lesquin ☎ 20 97 92 02
             ② **Novotel Lille Aéroport** LLL 59810 Lesquin ☎ 20 97 92 25
             ③ **Climat de France** L 59155 Faches-Thumesnil ☎ 20 97 00 24
Garages   ④ **Succursale** (Renault) ⑤ **Flandres Autos Sud** (Ford) ⑥ **Mercedes**
Banques   ⑦ **Crédit du Nord** ⑧ **Société Générale**
S/marché ⑨ **Noreco**

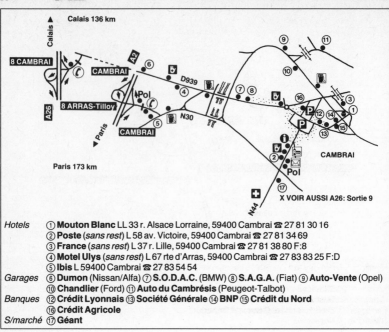

Hotels   ① **Mouton Blanc** LL 33 r. Alsace Lorraine, 59400 Cambrai ☎ 27 81 30 16
          ② **Poste** (*sans rest*) L 58 av. Victoire, 59400 Cambrai ☎ 27 81 34 69
          ③ **France** (*sans rest*) L 37 r. Lille, 59400 Cambrai ☎ 27 81 38 80 F:8
          ④ **Motel Ulys** (*sans rest*) L 67 rte d'Arras, 59400 Cambrai ☎ 27 83 83 25 F:D
          ⑤ **Ibis** L 59400 Cambrai ☎ 27 83 54 54
Garages   ⑥ **Dumon** (Nissan/Alfa) ⑦ **S.O.D.A.C.** (BMW) ⑧ **S.A.G.A.** (Fiat) ⑨ **Auto-Vente** (Opel)
          ⑩ **Chandlier** (Ford) ⑪ **Auto du Cambrésis** (Peugeot-Talbot)
Banques   ⑫ **Crédit Lyonnais** ⑬ **Société Générale** ⑭ **BNP** ⑮ **Crédit du Nord**
          ⑯ **Crédit Agricole**
S/marché ⑰ **Géant**

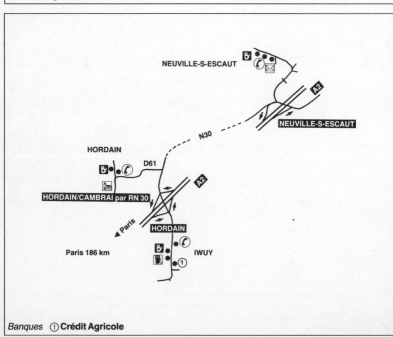

Banques   ① **Crédit Agricole**

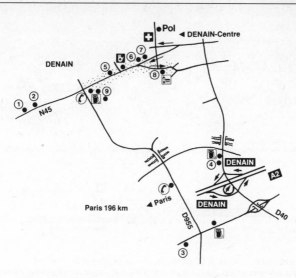

Garages ① **EAS** (Opel) ② **SO.DE.NA.** (Peugeot-Talbot) ③ **Hainaut Bretagne** (Renault)
④ **Relais de Thonville** (Ford)
Banques ⑤ **BNP** ⑥ **Société Générale** ⑦ **Crédit Lyonnais** ⑧ **Banque Populaire**
S/marché ⑨ **Carrefour**

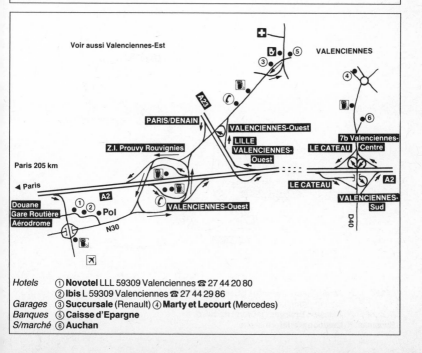

Hotels ① **Novotel** LLL 59309 Valenciennes ☎ 27 44 20 80
② **Ibis** L 59309 Valenciennes ☎ 27 44 29 86
Garages ③ **Succursale** (Renault) ④ **Marty et Lecourt** (Mercedes)
Banques ⑤ **Caisse d'Epargne**
S/marché ⑥ **Auchan**

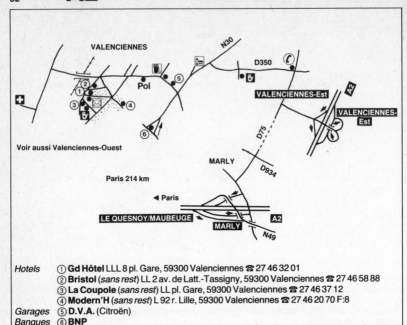

Hotels　　① **Gd Hôtel** LLL 8 pl. Gare, 59300 Valenciennes ☎ 27 46 32 01
　　　　　② **Bristol** (*sans rest*) LL 2 av. de Latt.-Tassigny, 59300 Valenciennes ☎ 27 46 58 88
　　　　　③ **La Coupole** (*sans rest*) LL pl. Gare, 59300 Valenciennes ☎ 27 46 37 12
　　　　　④ **Modern'H** (*sans rest*) L 92 r. Lille, 59300 Valenciennes ☎ 27 46 20 70 F:8
Garages　⑤ **D.V.A.** (Citroën)
Banques　⑥ **BNP**

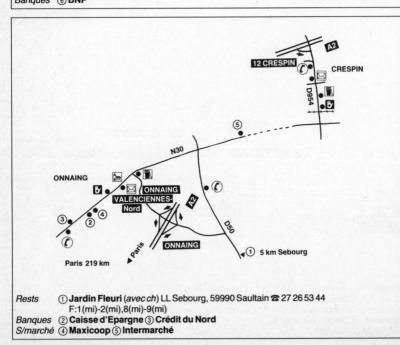

Rests　　① **Jardin Fleuri** (*avec ch*) LL Sebourg, 59990 Saultain ☎ 27 26 53 44
　　　　　F:1(mi)-2(mi),8(mi)-9(mi)
Banques　② **Caisse d'Epargne** ③ **Crédit du Nord**
S/marché　④ **Maxicoop** ⑤ **Intermarché**

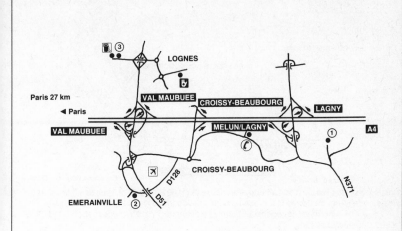

Hotels ① **Novotel** LLL 77206 Marne-la-Vallée ☎ (1) 60 05 91 15
② **Climat de France** L Emerainville, 77200 Torcy ☎ (1) 60 06 38 34
Garages ③ **Bries des Nations** (Renault)

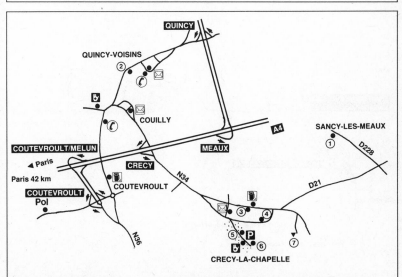

Hotels ① **La Catounière** LL Sancy-lès-Meaux, 77580 Crécy-la-Chapelle ☎ (1) 60 25 71 74
F:8,11
Garages ② **Demi Lune** (Citroën) ③ **Guillaumy** (Peugeot-Talbot) ④ **Moderne** (Renault)
Banques ⑤ **Crédit Agricole** ⑥ **Société Générale**
Camping ⑦ **Le Pré St-Jean** 77580 Crécy-la-Chapelle ☎ (1) 60 04 78 75

Hotels ① **Bec Fin** L 77260 La Ferté-s/s-Jouarre ☎ (1) 60 22 01 27 F:2,8(mi)-9(mi),Ma(s),Me
Rests ② **Aub. de Condé** LLL 77260 La Ferté-s/s-Jouarre ☎ (1) 60 22 00 07 F:2,L(s),Ma
③ **Le Gonfalon** (*avec ch*) LLL Germigny-l'Evêque, 77910 Varreddes ☎ (1) 60 25 29 29 F:1
Garages ④ **SOGAL** (Renault) ⑤ **Garage du Parc** (Citroën) ⑥ **Interauto** (Audi/VW)
Banques ⑦ **BNP** ⑧ **Crédit Lyonnais**
S/marché ⑨ **Maxicoop** ⑩ **Intermarché**
Camping ⑪ **Le Choisel** 77750 St-Cyr-sur-Morin ☎ (1) 60 23 84 93 F:11-2
⑫ **Les Bondons** 77260 La Ferté-s/s-Jouarre ☎ (1) 60 22 00 23
⑬ **L'Ile du Bac** 77910 Varreddes ☎ (1) 64 34 80 80

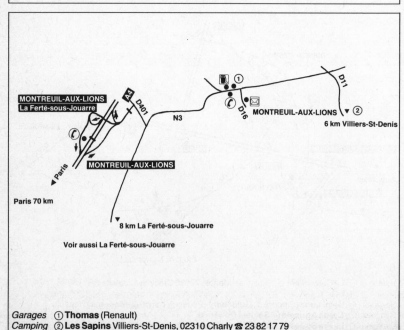

Garages ① **Thomas** (Renault)
Camping ② **Les Sapins** Villiers-St-Denis, 02310 Charly ☎ 23 82 17 79

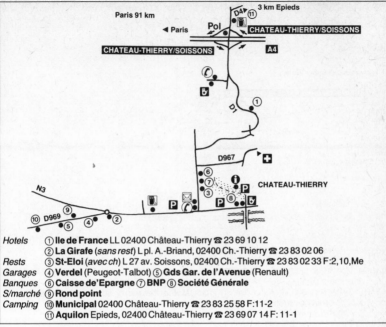

Paris 91 km

◄ Paris

Pol

D4► ⑪ 3 km Epieds

CHATEAU-THIERRY/SOISSONS

CHATEAU-THIERRY/SOISSONS

A4

D1

①

D967

CHATEAU-THIERRY

⑥
⑦
③
⑧

P

N3

⑩ D969 ⑨ ④ ② ⑤

Hotels	① **Ile de France** LL 02400 Château-Thierry ☎ 23 69 10 12
	② **La Girafe** (*sans rest*) L pl. A.-Briand, 02400 Ch.-Thierry ☎ 23 83 02 06
Rests	③ **St-Eloi** (*avec ch*) L 27 av. Soissons, 02400 Ch.-Thierry ☎ 23 83 02 33 F:2,10,Me
Garages	④ **Verdel** (Peugeot-Talbot) ⑤ **Gds Gar. de l'Avenue** (Renault)
Banques	⑥ **Caisse de l'Epargne** ⑦ **BNP** ⑧ **Société Générale**
S/marché	⑨ **Rond point**
Camping	⑩ **Municipal** 02400 Château-Thierry ☎ 23 83 25 58 F:11-2
	⑪ **Aquilon** Epieds, 02400 Château-Thierry ☎ 23 69 07 14 F: 11-1

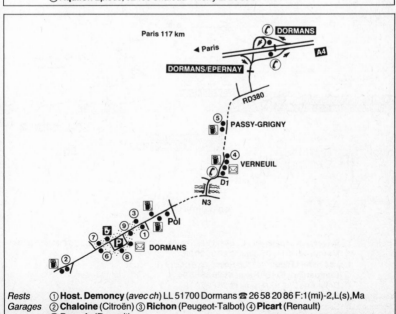

Paris 117 km

◄ Paris

DORMANS

DORMANS/EPERNAY

A4

RD380

⑤ PASSY-GRIGNY

④ VERNEUIL

D1

N3

③
⑨
⑦ Pol
①
⑥ ⑧ DORMANS

②

Rests	① **Host. Demoncy** (*avec ch*) LL 51700 Dormans ☎ 26 58 20 86 F:1(mi)-2,L(s),Ma
Garages	② **Chaloine** (Citroën) ③ **Richon** (Peugeot-Talbot) ④ **Picart** (Renault)
	⑤ **Beaude** (Renault)
Banques	⑥ **Caisse d'Epargne** ⑦ **Crédit Lyonnais** ⑧ **Crédit Agricole** ⑨ **Banque Populaire**

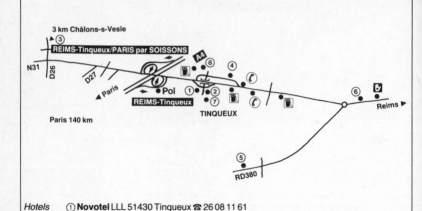

Hotels
- ① **Novotel** LLL 51430 Tinqueux ☎ 26 08 11 61
- ② **Ibis** L 51430 Tinqueux ☎ 26 04 60 70

Rests
- ③ **Assiette Champenoise** LLL Châlons-s-Vesle, 51140 Jonchery-s-Vesle ☎ 26 49 34 94 F:2,D(s),Me

Garages ④ **S.N.G.G.C.** (Peugeot-Talbot) ⑤ **Gar. Moine** (Renault) ⑥ **Succursale** (Citroën)

Banques ⑦ **Crédit Agricole**

S/marché ⑧ **Euromarché**

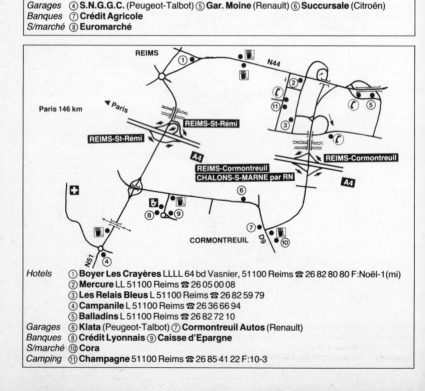

Hotels
- ① **Boyer Les Crayères** LLLLL 64 bd Vasnier, 51100 Reims ☎ 26 82 80 80 F:Noël-1(mi)
- ② **Mercure** LL 51100 Reims ☎ 26 05 00 08
- ③ **Les Relais Bleus** L 51100 Reims ☎ 26 82 59 79
- ④ **Campanile** L 51100 Reims ☎ 26 36 66 94
- ⑤ **Balladins** L 51100 Reims ☎ 26 82 72 10

Garages ⑥ **Klata** (Peugeot-Talbot) ⑦ **Cormontreuil Autos** (Renault)

Banques ⑧ **Crédit Lyonnais** ⑨ **Caisse d'Epargne**

S/marché ⑩ **Cora**

Camping ⑪ **Champagne** 51100 Reims ☎ 26 85 41 22 F:10-3

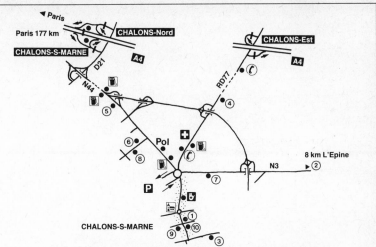

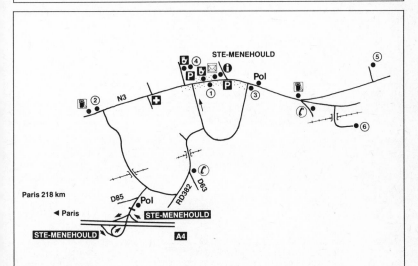

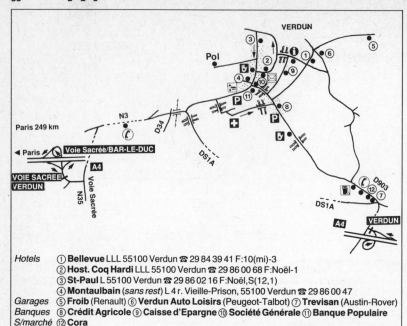

Hotels
   ① **Bellevue** LLL 55100 Verdun ☎ 29 84 39 41 F:10(mi)-3
   ② **Host. Coq Hardi** LLL 55100 Verdun ☎ 29 86 00 68 F:Noël-1
   ③ **St-Paul** L 55100 Verdun ☎ 29 86 02 16 F:Noël,S(12,1)
   ④ **Montaulbain** (*sans rest*) L 4 r. Vieille-Prison, 55100 Verdun ☎ 29 86 00 47
Garages ⑤ **Froib** (Renault) ⑥ **Verdun Auto Loisirs** (Peugeot-Talbot) ⑦ **Trevisan** (Austin-Rover)
Banques ⑧ **Crédit Agricole** ⑨ **Caisse d'Epargne** ⑩ **Société Générale** ⑪ **Banque Populaire**
S/marché ⑫ **Cora**

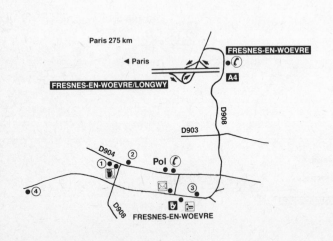

Garages ① **Havette & Drion**(Renault)
Banques ② **Caisse d'Epargne** ③ **Crédit Agricole**
Camping ④ **Base de Loisirs du Col Vert** Bonzée-en-Woëvre, 55160 Fresnes-en-Woëvre
   ☎ 29 87 31 98 F:10-3

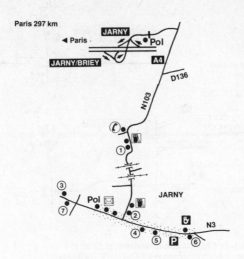

Garages ① **De Menech** (Toyota) ② **Rouy** (Citroën) ③ **Leclerc** (Renault)
Banques ④ **Crédit Agricole** ⑤ **Crédit Mutuel** ⑥ **Société Générale**
S/marché ⑦ **Intermarché**

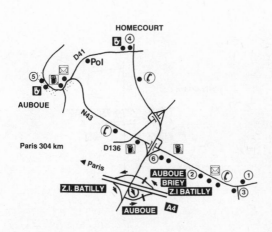

Garages ① **Bortot** (Renault)
Banques ② **Crédit Agricole** ③ **Caisse d'Epargne** ④ **Crédit Agricole** ⑤ **Caisse d'Epargne**
S/marché ⑥ **Cora**

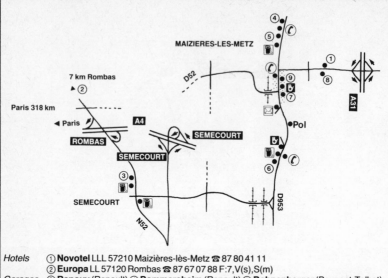

Hotels   ① **Novotel** LLL 57210 Maizières-lès-Metz ☎ 87 80 41 11
         ② **Europa** LL 57120 Rombas ☎ 87 67 07 88 F:7,V(s),S(m)
Garages   ③ **Repovy** (Renault) ④ **Bommersheim** (Renault) ⑤ **Bohnenberger** (Peugeot-Talbot)
         ⑥ **Magra** (Citroën)
Banques   ⑦ **Crédit Lyonnais**
S/marché   ⑧ **Leclerc** ⑨ **Super U**

Hotels   ① **La Bergerie** LL Rugy, 57640 Argancy ☎ 87 77 82 27

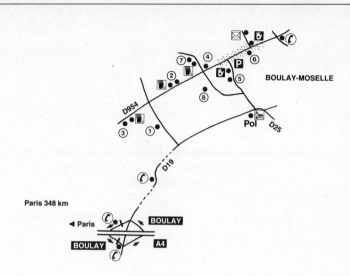

Garages ① **Garage ZF** (Ford) ② **Schwenke** (Renault) ③ **Antar** (Peugeot-Talbot)
Banques ④ **Caisse d'Epargne** ⑤ **BNP** ⑥ **Crédit Agricole**
S/marché ⑦ **Intermarché** ⑧ **Samest**

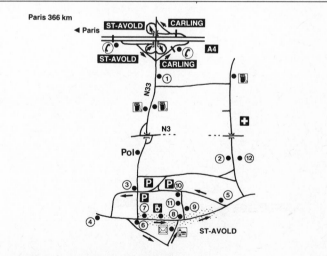

Hotels ① **Novotel** LLL 57500 St-Avold ☎ 87 92 25 93
② **Europe** LL 57500 St-Avold ☎ 87 92 00 33
Garages ③ **Pierrard** (Renault) ④ **Epin-Auto** (Peugeot-Talbot) ⑤ **du Centre** (Audi/VW)
Banques ⑥ **Caisse d'Epargne** ⑦ **Crédit Lyonnais** ⑧ **Barclays** ⑨ **Banque Populaire** ⑩ **BNP**
⑪ **Crédit Agricole**
S/marché ⑫ **Record**

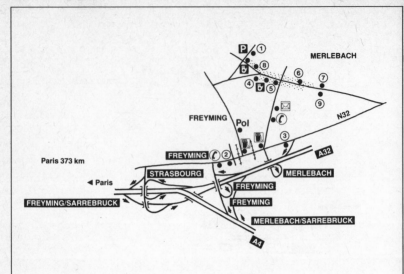

Hotels   ① **Caveau de la Bière** L 57800 Freyming-Merlebach ☎ 87 81 33 45 F:S,D(s)
Garages   ② **Derr** (Peugeot-Talbot) ③ **Spannagel** (Renault)
Banques   ④ **Crédit Agricole** ⑤ **Crédit Lyonnais** ⑥ **Caisse d'Epargne** ⑦ **Banque Populaire**
S/marché   ⑧ **Suma** ⑨ **Rond point**

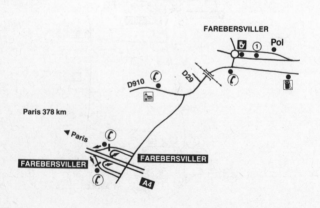

S/marché   ① **Champion**

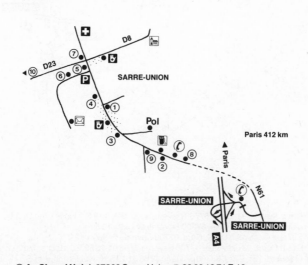

Hotels ① **Alsace** LLL 57200 Sarreguemines ☎ 87 98 44 32
② **Union** LL 57200 Sarreguemines ☎ 87 95 28 42
③ **Deux Etoiles** (*sans rest*) L 57200 Sarreguemines ☎ 87 98 46 32
Garages ④ **Meyer** (BMW) ⑤ **Niederlender** (Audi/VW) ⑥ **Martin Clus** (Ford) ⑦ **Fournier** (Renault)
⑧ **Bang** (Renault)
Banques ⑨ **Crédit Agricole** ⑩ **Société Générale** ⑪ **Crédit Lyonnais** ⑫ **Banque Populaire**
S/marché ⑬ **Unico**

Hotels ① **Au Cheval Noir** L 67260 Sarre-Union ☎ 88 00 12 71 F:10
Garages ② **Stutzmann** (Citroën) ③ **Schoepfer** (Renault)
Banques ④ **Caisse d'Epargne** ⑤ **Société Générale** ⑥ **Crédit Agricole** ⑦ **Banque Populaire**
S/marché ⑧ **Intermarché** ⑨ **Migros**
Camping ⑩ **Mun. de l'Etang** Harskirchen, 67260 Sarre-Union ☎ 88 00 93 65

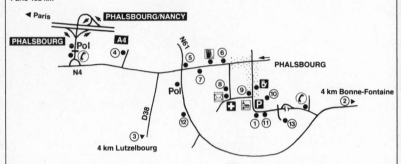

Hotels
① **Erckmann-Chatrian** LL 57370 Phalsbourg ☎ 87 24 31 33 F:10
② **Notre-Dame** LL Bonne-Fontaine, 57370 Phalsbourg ☎ 87 24 34 33 F:1,2,V
③ **Vosges** L 57820 Lutzelbourg ☎ 87 25 30 09 F:1(mi)-3(mi),Me
Garages ④ **Tromp** (Renault) ⑤ **Wetzel** (Citroën) ⑥ **Klein** (Peugeot-Talbot) ⑦ **Dene** (Fiat)
Banques ⑧ **Caisse d'Epargne** ⑨ **Crédit Agricole** ⑩ **Crédit Mutuel** ⑪ **Banque Populaire**
S/marché ⑫ **Maxicoop**
Camping ⑬ **Municipal du Vieux Château** 57370 Phalsbourg ☎ 87 24 13 72 F:11-3

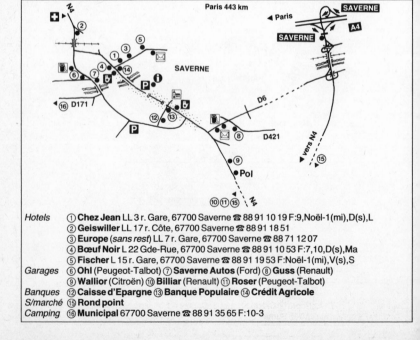

Hotels
① **Chez Jean** LL 3 r. Gare, 67700 Saverne ☎ 88 91 10 19 F:9,Noël-1(mi),D(s),L
② **Geiswiller** LL 17 r. Côte, 67700 Saverne ☎ 88 91 18 51
③ **Europe** (sans rest) LL 7 r. Gare, 67700 Saverne ☎ 88 71 12 07
④ **Bœuf Noir** L 22 Gde-Rue, 67700 Saverne ☎ 88 91 10 53 F:7,10,D(s),Ma
⑤ **Fischer** L 15 r. Gare, 67700 Saverne ☎ 88 91 19 53 F:Noël-1(mi),V(s),S
Garages ⑥ **Ohl** (Peugeot-Talbot) ⑦ **Saverne Autos** (Ford) ⑧ **Guss** (Renault)
⑨ **Wallior** (Citroën) ⑩ **Billiar** (Renault) ⑪ **Roser** (Peugeot-Talbot)
Banques ⑫ **Caisse d'Epargne** ⑬ **Banque Populaire** ⑭ **Crédit Agricole**
S/marché ⑮ **Rond point**
Camping ⑯ **Municipal** 67700 Saverne ☎ 88 91 35 65 F:10-3

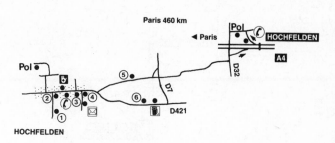

Garages ① **Hammann** (Renault)
Banques ② **Crédit Mutuel** ③ **Crédit Agricole** ④ **Caisse d'Epargne**
S/marché ⑤ **Coop** ⑥ **Migros**

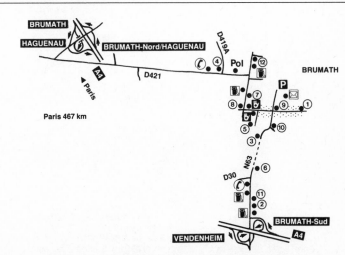

Hotels ① **Ville de Paris** L 67170 Brumath ☎ 88 51 11 02 F:6(mi)-7(mi),D(s),V
② **Grittwald** L 67170 Brumath ☎ 88 51 09 44
Rests ③ **Ecrevisse** (*avec ch*) L 67170 Brumath ☎ 88 51 11 08 F:1,7(mi)-8(mi),L(s),Ma
Garages ④ **Gar. Pierre** (Peugeot-Talbot) ⑤ **Gar. Weibel** (Ford) ⑥ **Goetz** (Renault)
Banques ⑦ **Crédit Agricole** ⑧ **Crédit Mutuel** ⑨ **Caisse d'Epargne** ⑩ **Banque Populaire**
S/marché ⑪ **Intermarché** ⑫ **Suma**

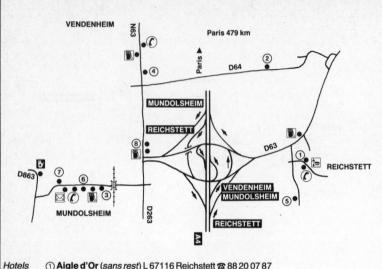

Hotels ① **Aigle d'Or** (*sans rest*) L 67116 Reichstett ☎ 88 20 07 87
Rests ② **Auberge de la Forêt** (*avec ch*) L 67550 ☎ 88 20 01 15
Garages ③ **Schopf** (Peugeot-Talbot) ④ **Renault**
Banques ⑤ **Crédit Agricole** ⑥ **Caisse d'Epargne** ⑦ **Crédit Agricole**
S/marché ⑧ **Cora**

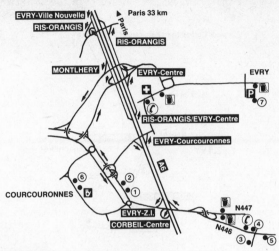

Hotels ① **Novotel Paris Evry** LLL 91021 Evry Cedex ☎ (1) 60 77 82 70
　　　　 ② **Ibis** L 91021 Evry Cedex ☎ (1) 60 77 74 75
　　　　 ③ **Campanile** L 91100 Corbeil-Essonnes ☎ (1) 60 89 41 45
Garages ④ **Féray** (Renault) ⑤ **Corbeil-Essonnes Auto** (Citroën)
Banques ⑥ **BNP**
S/marché ⑦ **Euromarché**

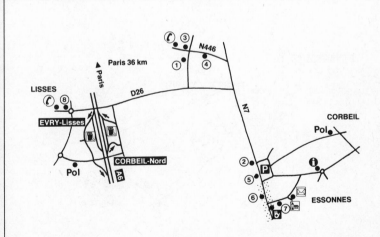

Hotels ① **Campanile** L 91100 Corbeil-Essonnes ☎ (1) 60 89 41 45
Rests   ② **Aux Armes de France** (*avec ch*) LL 91100 Essonnes ☎ (1) 64 96 24 04 F:8
Garages ③ **Féray** (Renault) ④ **Corbeil-Essonnes Auto** (Citroën) ⑤ **Bertrand Auto** (Alfa)
Banques ⑥ **Crédit Lyonnais** ⑦ **Banque Populaire**
S/marché ⑧ **Intermarché**

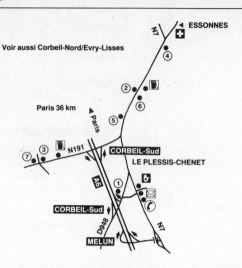

Voir aussi Corbeil-Nord/Evry-Lisses

Paris 36 km

Hotels ① **Climat de France** L 91830 Le Coudray-Montceaux ☎ (1) 64 93 85 36
Garages ② **Européen** (Volvo) ③ **Barbaray** (Renault) ④ **Desrues** (Peugeot-Talbot)
⑤ **Vachon** (BMW) ⑥ **Corbeil-Autos** (Fiat)
S/marché ⑦ **Intermarché**

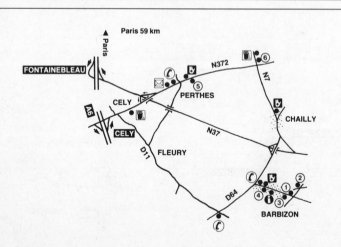

Hotels ① **Bas-Bréau** LLLL 77630 Barbizon ☎ (1) 60 66 40 05 F:1-2(mi)
② **Les Alouettes** LL 77630 Barbizon ☎ (1) 60 66 41 98
Rests ③ **Les Pléiades** (*avec ch*) LLL 77630 Barbizon ☎ (1) 60 66 40 25
④ **Clé d'Or** (*avec ch*) LLL 77630 Barbizon ☎ (1) 60 66 40 96 F:11(mi)-12(mi), D(s), L
Garages ⑤ **Mercier** (Citroën)
S/marché ⑥ **Carrefour**

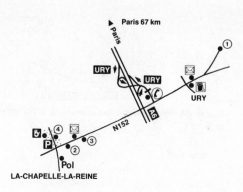

Hotels   ① **Novotel** LLL 77116 Ury ☎ (1) 64 22 48 25
Garages   ② **Moulin** (Renault) ③ **Nieutin** (Citroën)
Banques   ④ **Crédit Agricole**

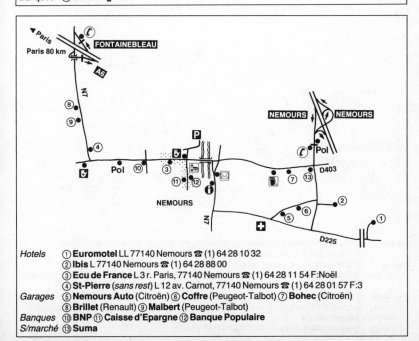

Hotels   ① **Euromotel** LL 77140 Nemours ☎ (1) 64 28 10 32
          ② **Ibis** L 77140 Nemours ☎ (1) 64 28 88 00
          ③ **Ecu de France** L 3 r. Paris, 77140 Nemours ☎ (1) 64 28 11 54 F:Noël
          ④ **St-Pierre** (*sans rest*) L 12 av. Carnot, 77140 Nemours ☎ (1) 64 28 01 57 F:3
Garages   ⑤ **Nemours Auto** (Citroën) ⑥ **Coffre** (Peugeot-Talbot) ⑦ **Bohec** (Citroën)
          ⑧ **Brillet** (Renault) ⑨ **Malbert** (Peugeot-Talbot)
Banques   ⑩ **BNP** ⑪ **Caisse d'Epargne** ⑫ **Banque Populaire**
S/marché ⑬ **Suma**

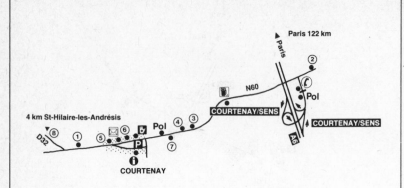

Rests   ① **Le Relais** (*avec ch*) L 45320 Courtenay ☎ 38 97 41 60 F:1, 11, D(s), L
Garages   ② **Chapuis** (Renault) ③ **Courtenay** (Peugeot-Talbot) ④ **Meunier** (Citroën)
Banques   ⑤ **Banque Populaire** ⑥ **Société Générale**
S/marché ⑦ **Maxi-Marché**
Camping ⑧ **Intercommunal** St-Hilaire-les-Andrésis, 45320 Courtenay ☎ 38 97 00 75 F:9(mi)-5

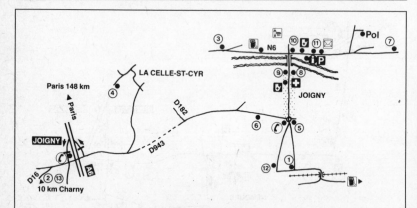

Hotels   ① **Modern'H Frères Godard** LLL 89300 Joigny ☎ 86 62 16 28 F:11(mi)-12(mi)
        ② **Gare** L 89120 Charny ☎ 86 63 61 59 F:9, 12(mi)-1(mi), D(s), L
Rests   ③ **A la Côte St-Jacques** (*avec ch*) LLLL 89300 Joigny ☎ 86 62 09 70 F:1-2(mi)
       ④ **Fontaine aux Muses** (*avec ch*) LL 89970 La Celle-St-Cyr ☎ 86 73 40 22 F:L, Ma(m)
       ⑤ **Paris Nice** (*avec ch*) L 89300 Joigny ☎ 86 62 06 72 F:1, D(s), L
Garages   ⑥ **Fournet** (Audi/VW) ⑦ **S.A.J.A.** (Renault)
Banques   **Caisse d'Epargne** ⑨ **Société Générale** ⑩ **Crédit Lyonnais** ⑪ **Banque Populaire**
S/marché ⑫ **Intermarché**
Camping ⑬ **Municipal le Pâtis** 89120 Charny F:10-3(mi)

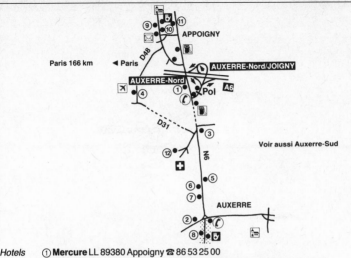

Hotels   ① **Mercure** LL 89380 Appoigny ☎ 86 53 25 00
             ② **Normandie** (*sans rest*) LL 41 bd Vauban, 89000 Auxerre ☎ 86 52 57 80
             ③ **Les Clarions** LL 89000 Auxerre ☎ 86 46 85 64
             ④ **Les Bruyères** LL 89000 Auxerre ☎ 86 53 07 22 F:11-2, D(s)
Garages   ⑤ **Caratte** (Volvo) ⑥ **Rte de Paris** (Peugeot-Talbot) ⑦ **Europe-Auto** (Mercedes)
Banques   ⑧ **Banque de la Henin** ⑨ **Caisse d'Epargne** ⑩ **Crédit Agricole**
S/marché   ⑪ **Maxicoop** ⑫ **As-Eco**

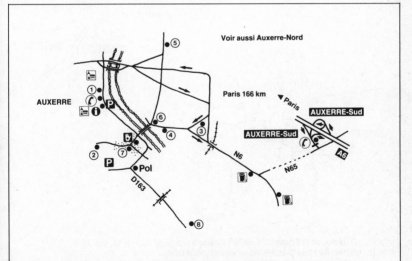

Hotels   ① **Le Maxime** LLL 2 quai Marine, 89000 Auxerre ☎ 86 52 14 19
             ② **Seignelay** L 2 r. Pont, 89000 Auxerre ☎ 86 52 03 48 F:1-2(mi), L(10-7)
Garages   ③ **Jules Ferry** (Alfa) ④ **Gambetta** (Ford) ⑤ **SODIVA** (Renault)
Banques   ⑥ **BNP** ⑦ **Crédit Agricole**
Camping   ⑧ **Municipal** 8 rte de Vaux, 89000 Auxerre ☎ 86 52 11 15 F:11-3

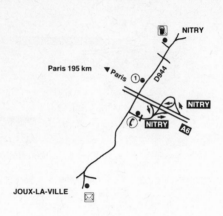

Hotels   ① **Paillotel** (*sans rest*) L 89310 Nitry ☎ 86 33 64 33

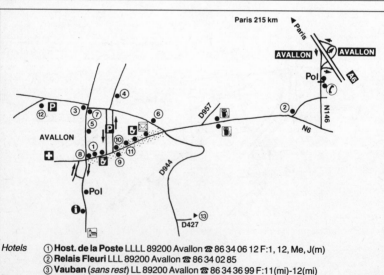

Hotels   ① **Host. de la Poste** LLLLL 89200 Avallon ☎ 86 34 06 12 F:1, 12, Me, J(m)
     ② **Relais Fleuri** LLLL 89200 Avallon ☎ 86 34 02 85
     ③ **Vauban** (*sans rest*) LL 89200 Avallon ☎ 86 34 36 99 F:11(mi)-12(mi)
Rests   ④ **Les Capucins** (*avec ch*) LL 89200 Avallon ☎ 86 34 06 52 F:6,12(mi)-1(mi),Ma(s),Me
Garages   ⑤ **Gueneau** (Renault) ⑥ **Michot** (Citroën)
Banques   ⑦ **Banque Populaire** ⑧ **BNP** ⑨ **Crédit Agricole** ⑩ **Soc. Gén.** ⑪ **Crédit Lyonnais**
S/marché   ⑫ **Suma**
Camping   ⑬ **Municipal de Sous-Roche** 89200 Avallon ☎ 86 34 10 39 F:10(mi)-3(mi)

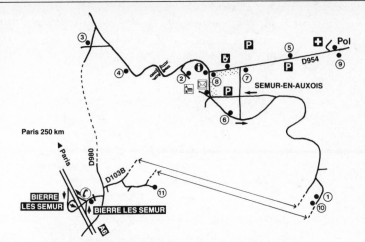

Hotels	① **Lac** LL 21140 Semur-en-Auxois ☎ 80 97 11 11 F:12(mi)-1, D(s), L
	② **Gourmets** L 21140 Semur-en-Auxois ☎ 80 97 09 41 F:11, 12, Ma
Garages	③ **Jarno** (Citroën) ④ **Delaveau** (Ford) ⑤ **Girard** (Renault)
Banques	⑥ **Banque Populaire** ⑦ **Crédit Agricole** ⑧ **Crédit Mutuel**
S/marché	⑨ **Suma**
Camping	⑩ **Municipal du Lac de Pont** 21140 Semur-en-Auxois ☎ 80 97 01 26 F:10-4
	⑪ **Camp V.V.F.** 21140 Semur-en-Auxois ☎ 80 97 12 99 F:11-4(mi)

Hotels	① **Motel Val Vert** (*sans rest*) LL 21320 Pouilly-en-Auxois ☎ 80 90 82 34
	② **Poste** (*sans rest*) L 21230 Arnay-le-Duc ☎ 80 90 00 76 F:10-5
Rests	③ **Chez Camille** (*avec ch*) LLL 21230 Arnay-le-Duc ☎ 80 90 01 38 F:1
	④ **Terminus** (*avec ch*) L 21230 Arnay-le-Duc ☎ 80 90 00 33 F:1-2(mi), Me
Garages	⑤ **Orset** (Renault) ⑥ **Gar. de l'Autoroute** (Citroën) ⑦ **Jeannin** (Peugeot-Talbot)
Banques	⑧ **Caisse d'Epargne** ⑨ **Banque Populaire**
S/marché	⑩ **Maxi Marché**
Camping	⑪ **Municipal le Vert Auxois** 21320 Pouilly-en-Auxois F:10-4
	⑫ **Municipal de Fouché** 21230 Arnay-le-Duc ☎ 80 90 02 23

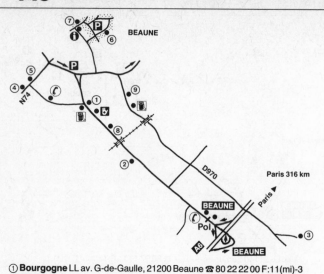

Hotels ① **Bourgogne** LL av. G-de-Gaulle, 21200 Beaune ☎ 80 22 22 00 F:11(mi)-3
        ② **Climat de France** L Z.A. de la Chartreuse, 21200 Beaune ☎ 80 22 74 10
        ③ **Parc** (*sans rest*) L Levernois, 21200 Beaune ☎ 80 22 22 51 F:11(mi)-12(mi), 3
Garages ④ **Champion** (Citroën) ⑤ **Bolatre** (Fiat)
Banques ⑥ **BNP** ⑦ **Banque Populaire**
S/marché ⑧ **Rond point** ⑨ **Suma**

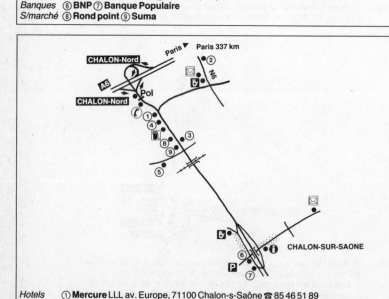

Hotels ① **Mercure** LLL av. Europe, 71100 Chalon-s-Saône ☎ 85 46 51 89
        ② **Climat de France** L Champforgeuil, 71100 Chalon-s-Saône ☎ 85 46 40 04
        ③ **Ibis** (*sans rest*) L av. Europe, 71100 Chalon-s-Saône ☎ 85 46 64 62
Garages ④ **Sodirac** (Renault) ⑤ **Moderne** (Citroën)
Banques ⑥ **C.C.F.** ⑦ **Banque Populaire**
S/marché ⑧ **Mammouth** ⑨ **Conforama**

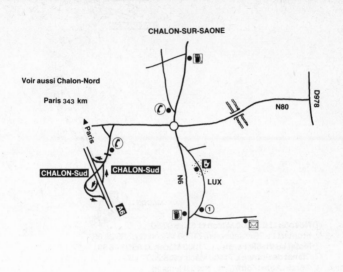

CHALON-SUR-SAONE

Voir aussi Chalon-Nord

Paris 343 km

N80

D978

Paris

CHALON-Sud   **CHALON-Sud**

A6

N6

LUX

Hotels ① **Charmilles** LL Lux, 71100 Chalon-s-Saône ☎ 85 48 58 08

TOURNUS   Paris ▶   Paris 365 km

A6

TOURNUS

③

N6

⑤   ⑥

④

Pol   ①   **TOURNUS**

②

⑦

Hotels ① **Le Rempart** LLL 2 av. Gambetta, 71700 Tournus ☎ 85 51 10 56
② **Le Sauvage** LL pl. Champ-de-Mars, 71700 Tournus ☎ 85 51 14 45 F:11(mi)-12(mi)
③ **Motel Clos Mouron** (*sans rest*) L 71700 Tournus ☎ 85 51 23 86 F:Noël, D(10-4)
Rests ④ **Greuze** LLL 71700 Tournus ☎ 85 51 13 52 F:11(mi)-12(mi), J
Garages ⑤ **Pageaud** (Renault) ⑥ **Guillemaut** (Citroën)
Banques ⑦ **Crédit Agricole**

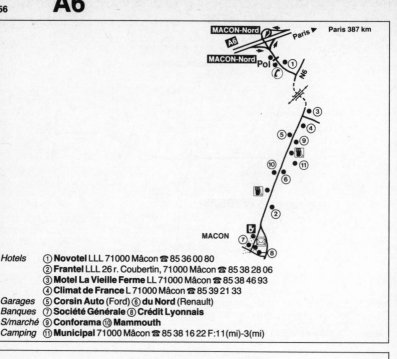

Hotels	① **Novotel** LLL 71000 Mâcon ☎ 85 36 00 80
	② **Frantel** LLL 26 r. Coubertin, 71000 Mâcon ☎ 85 38 28 06
	③ **Motel La Vieille Ferme** LL 71000 Mâcon ☎ 85 38 46 93
	④ **Climat de France** L 71000 Mâcon ☎ 85 39 21 33
Garages	⑤ **Corsin Auto** (Ford) ⑥ **du Nord** (Renault)
Banques	⑦ **Société Générale** ⑧ **Crédit Lyonnais**
S/marché	⑨ **Conforama** ⑩ **Mammouth**
Camping	⑪ **Municipal** 71000 Mâcon ☎ 85 38 16 22 F:11(mi)-3(mi)

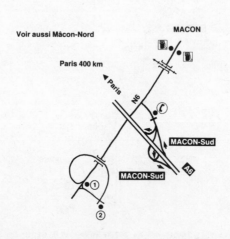

Hotels	① **Ibis** L 71570 Chaintré ☎ 85 36 51 60
S/marché	② **Carrefour**

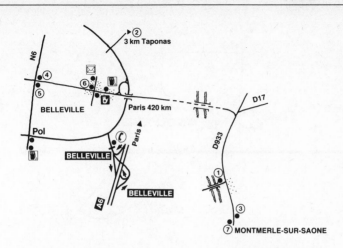

Hotels	① **Rivage** LL 01090 Montmerle-s-Saône ☎ 74 69 33 92 F:2, 11(mi)-12(mi), Me
	② **Aub. des Sablons** L Taponas, 69220 Belleville ☎ 74 66 34 80 F:2, Ma
Rests	③ **Castel de Valrose** (*avec ch*) LL 01090 Montmerle ☎ 74 69 30 52 F:1, D(s), L
Garages	④ **Dépérier** (Renault)
Banques	⑤ **BNP** ⑥ **Crédit Lyonnais**
Camping	⑦ **Municipal Sud** 01090 Montmerle-s-Saône ☎ 74 69 34 40 F:11-3

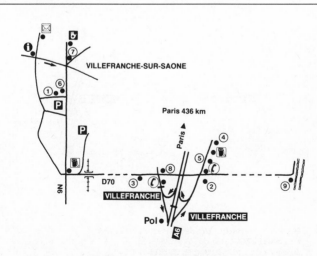

Hotels	① **Plaisance** LLL 96 av. Libération, 69400 Villefranche ☎ 74 65 33 52 F:Noël
	② **Ibis** L 69400 Villefranche-s-Saône ☎ 74 68 22 23
Garages	③ **Renault-Villefranche** (Renault) ④ **Gambetta** (Ford) ⑤ **Thivolle** (Citroën)
Banques	⑥ **Crédit Agricole** ⑦ **Caisse d'Epargne**
S/marché	⑧ **Intermarché**
Camping	⑨ **Municipal** 69400 Villefranche-s-Saône ☎ 74 65 33 48 F:10-4

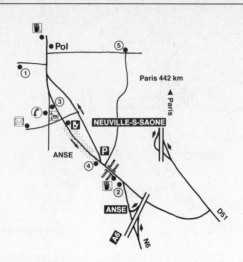

Hotels ① **St-Romain** LL rte Graves, 69480 Anse ☎ 74 68 05 89
Garages ② **F. Blanc** (Renault)
Banques ③ **Caisse d'Epargne** ④ **BNP**
Camping ⑤ **International Camping** 69480 Anse ☎ 74 67 00 68 F:10-4

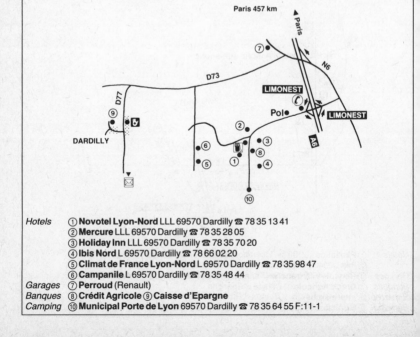

Hotels ① **Novotel Lyon-Nord** LLL 69570 Dardilly ☎ 78 35 13 41
② **Mercure** LLL 69570 Dardilly ☎ 78 35 28 05
③ **Holiday Inn** LLL 69570 Dardilly ☎ 78 35 70 20
④ **Ibis Nord** L 69570 Dardilly ☎ 78 66 02 20
⑤ **Climat de France Lyon-Nord** L 69570 Dardilly ☎ 78 35 98 47
⑥ **Campanile** L 69570 Dardilly ☎ 78 35 48 44
Garages ⑦ **Perroud** (Renault)
Banques ⑧ **Crédit Agricole** ⑨ **Caisse d'Epargne**
Camping ⑩ **Municipal Porte de Lyon** 69570 Dardilly ☎ 78 35 64 55 F:11-1

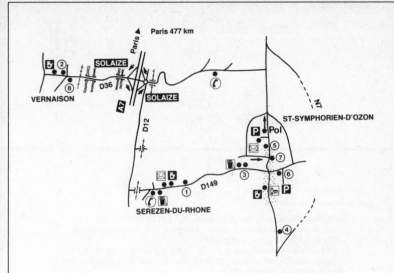

Hotels ① **La Bourbonnaise** LL Sérézin-du-Rhône, 69360 St-Symphorien ☎ 78 02 80 58
Garages ② **Ganivet-Clair** (Renault) ③ **Ollagnon** (Fiat) ④ **Beal** (Volvo)
Banques ⑤ **Caisse d'Epargne** ⑥ **Crédit Agricole** ⑦ **Crédit Lyonnais** ⑧ **Caisse d'Epargne**

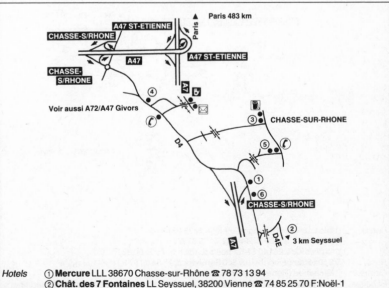

Hotels ① **Mercure** LLL 38670 Chasse-sur-Rhône ☎ 78 73 13 94
　　　　 ② **Chât. des 7 Fontaines** LL Seyssuel, 38200 Vienne ☎ 74 85 25 70 F:Noël-1
Garages ③ **Modern** (Renault)
Banques ④ **Crédit Agricole** ⑤ **Caisse d'Epargne**
S/marché ⑥ **Record**

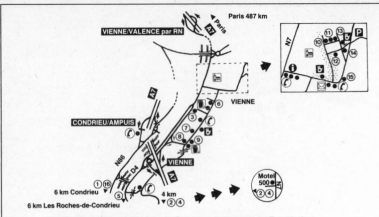

VIENNE/VALENCE par RN

CONDRIEU/AMPUIS

VIENNE

VIENNE

N86

N D4

6 km Condrieu
6 km Les Roches-de-Condrieu

4 km

Motel 500

Hotels	① **Hôt. Beau Rivage** LLL 69420 Condrieu ☎ 74 59 52 24 F:1-2(mi)
	② **Host. Marais St-Jean** LLL Chonas l'Amballan, 38121 Reventin-Vaugris ☎ 74 58 83 28 F:2-3(mi), Ma(s), Me
	③ **La Rés. de la Pyramide** *(sans rest)* LL 38200 Vienne ☎ 74 53 16 46 F:2,11
	④ **Domaine de Clairefontaine** L Chonas l'Amballan, 38121 Reventin-Vaugris ☎ 74 58 81 52 F:12-1,D(s), L(m)
	⑤ **Bellevue** LL 38370 Les Roches-de-Condrieu ☎ 74 56 41 42 F:2(mi)-3(mi), D(s), L
Garages	⑥ **Rhône** (Ren.) ⑦ **Central** (Ford) ⑧ **Barbier** (Peugeot-Talbot) ⑨ **Gévaudan** (Cit.)
Banques	⑩ **Créd. Lyonnais** ⑪ **Ban. Pop.** ⑫ **Créd. Ag.** ⑬ **BNP** ⑭ **Soc. Gén.** ⑮ **Caisse d'Ep.**
Camping	⑯ **Belle-Rive** 69420 Condrieu ☎ 74 59 51 08 F:10-3

▲ Paris   Paris 517 km

CHANAS/ST-RAMBERT-D'ALBON/ANNONAY

Pol   CHANAS/ANNONAY

SERRIÈRES   CHANAS

N82   N7   D519

ST-RAMBERT-D'ALBON

P

Pol

Hotels	① **Ibis** L 26140 St-Rambert-d'Albon ☎ 75 03 04 00
	② **Halte OK** L 38150 Chanas ☎ 74 29 87 50
	③ **Croix d'Or** L 26140 St-Rambert-d'Albon ☎ 75 31 00 35 F:2,8,J
Rests	④ **Schaeffer** *(avec ch)* L 07340 Serrières ☎ 75 34 00 07 F:Noël-1,L(s),Ma
Garages	⑤ **Michallon** (Renault) ⑥ **Ortega** (Renault)
Banques	⑦ **Crédit Lyonnais** ⑧ **Banque Populaire** ⑨ **Crédit Agricole** ⑩ **Société Générale**
S/marché	⑪ **Genty**
Camping	⑫ **Les Guyots** Chanas, 38150 Roussillon ☎ 74 84 20 09 F:10(mi)-3
	⑬ **Beauséjour** Chanas, 38150 Roussillon ☎ 74 84 31 01 F:10-3

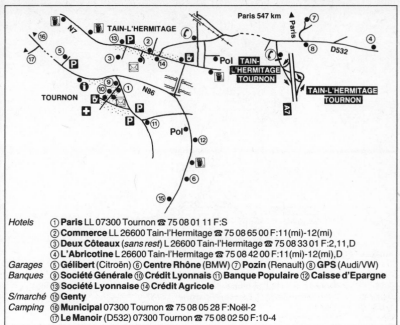

Hotels	
	① **Paris** LL 07300 Tournon ☎ 75 08 01 11 F:S
	② **Commerce** LL 26600 Tain-l'Hermitage ☎ 75 08 65 00 F:11(mi)-12(mi)
	③ **Deux Côteaux** (*sans rest*) L 26600 Tain-l'Hermitage ☎ 75 08 33 01 F:2,11,D
	④ **L'Abricotine** L 26600 Tain-l'Hermitage ☎ 75 08 42 00 F:11(mi)-12(mi),D
Garages	⑤ **Gélibert** (Citroën) ⑥ **Centre Rhône** (BMW) ⑦ **Pozin** (Renault) ⑧ **GPS** (Audi/VW)
Banques	⑨ **Société Générale** ⑩ **Crédit Lyonnais** ⑪ **Banque Populaire** ⑫ **Caisse d'Epargne**
	⑬ **Société Lyonnaise** ⑭ **Crédit Agricole**
S/marché	⑮ **Genty**
Camping	⑯ **Municipal** 07300 Tournon ☎ 75 08 05 28 F:Noël-2
	⑰ **Le Manoir** (D532) 07300 Tournon ☎ 75 08 02 50 F:10-4

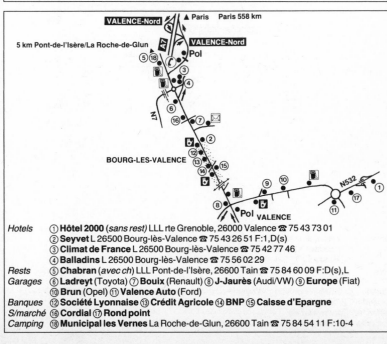

Hotels	
	① **Hôtel 2000** (*sans rest*) LLL rte Grenoble, 26000 Valence ☎ 75 43 73 01
	② **Seyvet** L 26500 Bourg-lès-Valence ☎ 75 43 26 51 F:1,D(s)
	③ **Climat de France** L 26500 Bourg-lès-Valence ☎ 75 42 77 46
	④ **Balladins** L 26500 Bourg-lès-Valence ☎ 75 56 02 29
Rests	⑤ **Chabran** (*avec ch*) LLL Pont-de-l'Isère, 26600 Tain ☎ 75 84 60 09 F:D(s),L
Garages	⑥ **Ladreyt** (Toyota) ⑦ **Bouix** (Renault) ⑧ **J-Jaurès** (Audi/VW) ⑨ **Europe** (Fiat)
	⑩ **Brun** (Opel) ⑪ **Valence Auto** (Ford)
Banques	⑫ **Société Lyonnaise** ⑬ **Crédit Agricole** ⑭ **BNP** ⑮ **Caisse d'Epargne**
S/marché	⑯ **Cordial** ⑰ **Rond point**
Camping	⑱ **Municipal les Vernes** La Roche-de-Glun, 26600 Tain ☎ 75 84 54 11 F:10-4

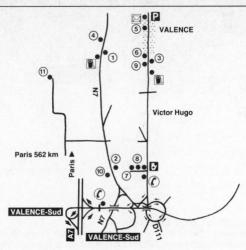

Hotels
① **Novotel** LLL 217 av. Provence, 26000 Valence ☎ 75 42 20 15
② **Ibis** L 355 av. Provence, 26000 Valence ☎ 75 44 42 54
Rests
③ **Pic** (avec ch) LLLL 285 av. V-Hugo, 26000 Valence ☎ 75 44 15 32 F:2,8,D(s),Me
Garages
④ **Royal** (Mercedes) ⑤ **Clauzier & Genin** (Audi/VW) ⑥ **SOVACA** (Peugeot-Talbot)
Banques
⑦ **Banque Populaire** ⑧ **Caisse d'Epargne** ⑨ **BNP**
S/marché
⑩ **Géant**
Camping
⑪ **L'Epervière** 26000 Valence ☎ 75 43 63 01 F:Noël

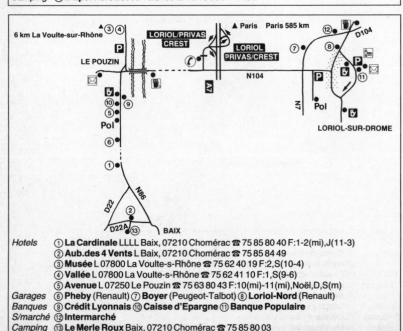

Hotels
① **La Cardinale** LLLL Baix, 07210 Chomérac ☎ 75 85 80 40 F:1-2(mi),J(11-3)
② **Aub. des 4 Vents** L Baix, 07210 Chomérac ☎ 75 85 84 49
③ **Musée** L 07800 La Voulte-s-Rhône ☎ 75 62 40 19 F:2,S(10-4)
④ **Vallée** L 07800 La Voulte-s-Rhône ☎ 75 62 41 10 F:1,S(9-6)
⑤ **Avenue** L 07250 Le Pouzin ☎ 75 63 80 43 F:10(mi)-11(mi),Noël,D,S(m)
Garages
⑥ **Pheby** (Renault) ⑦ **Boyer** (Peugeot-Talbot) ⑧ **Loriol-Nord** (Renault)
Banques
⑨ **Crédit Lyonnais** ⑩ **Caisse d'Epargne** ⑪ **Banque Populaire**
S/marché
⑫ **Intermarché**
Camping
⑬ **Le Merle Roux** Baix, 07210 Chomérac ☎ 75 85 80 03

Hotels	① **La Capitelle** L Mirmande, 26270 Loriol ☎ 75 63 02 72 F:11(mi)-2,Ma
	② **Ibis** L 26370 Saulce-sur-Rhône ☎ 75 63 09 60
	③ **Clutier/Les Reys de Saulce** L Saulce-s-Rhône, 26270 Loriol ☎ 75 63 00 22 F:12(mi)-1(mi),D(s),L
Garages	④ **Vignard** (Renault)
Banques	⑤ **Caisse d'Epargne**
Camping	⑥ **La Poche** Mirmande, 26270 Loriol ☎ 75 63 02 88 F:11-3

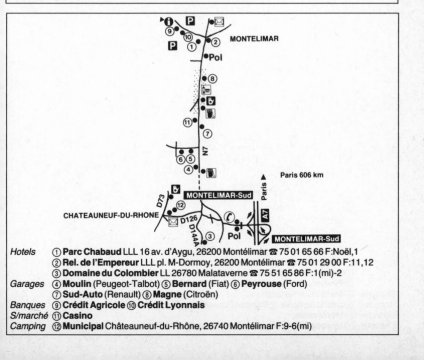

Hotels	① **Parc Chabaud** LLL 16 av. d'Aygu, 26200 Montélimar ☎ 75 01 65 66 F:Noël,1
	② **Rel. de l'Empereur** LLL pl. M-Dormoy, 26200 Montélimar ☎ 75 01 29 00 F:11,12
	③ **Domaine du Colombier** LL 26780 Malataverne ☎ 75 51 65 86 F:1(mi)-2
Garages	④ **Moulin** (Peugeot-Talbot) ⑤ **Bernard** (Fiat) ⑥ **Peyrouse** (Ford)
	⑦ **Sud-Auto** (Renault) ⑧ **Magne** (Citroën)
Banques	⑨ **Crédit Agricole** ⑩ **Crédit Lyonnais**
S/marché	⑪ **Casino**
Camping	⑫ **Municipal** Châteauneuf-du-Rhône, 26740 Montélimar F:9-6(mi)

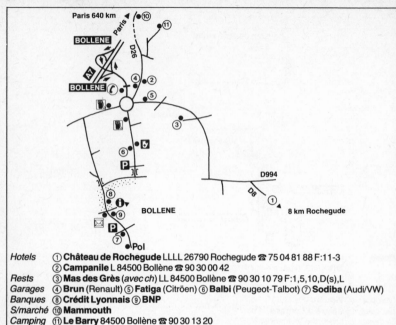

Hotels	① **Château de Rochegude** LLLL 26790 Rochegude ☎ 75 04 81 88 F:11-3
	② **Campanile** L 84500 Bollène ☎ 90 30 00 42
Rests	③ **Mas des Grès** (*avec ch*) LL 84500 Bollène ☎ 90 30 10 79 F:1,5,10,D(s),L
Garages	④ **Brun** (Renault) ⑤ **Fatiga** (Citröen) ⑥ **Balbi** (Peugeot-Talbot) ⑦ **Sodiba** (Audi/VW)
Banques	⑧ **Crédit Lyonnais** ⑨ **BNP**
S/marché	⑩ **Mammouth**
Camping	⑪ **Le Barry** 84500 Bollène ☎ 90 30 13 20

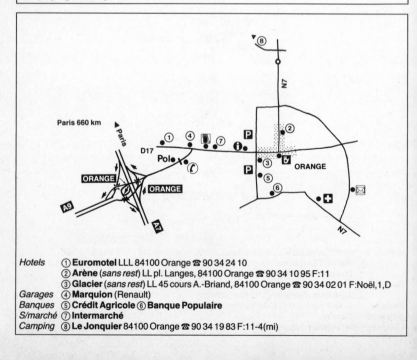

Hotels	① **Euromotel** LLL 84100 Orange ☎ 90 34 24 10
	② **Arène** (*sans rest*) LL pl. Langes, 84100 Orange ☎ 90 34 10 95 F:11
	③ **Glacier** (*sans rest*) LL 45 cours A.-Briand, 84100 Orange ☎ 90 34 02 01 F:Noël,1,D
Garages	④ **Marquion** (Renault)
Banques	⑤ **Crédit Agricole** ⑥ **Banque Populaire**
S/marché	⑦ **Intermarché**
Camping	⑧ **Le Jonquier** 84100 Orange ☎ 90 34 19 83 F:11-4(mi)

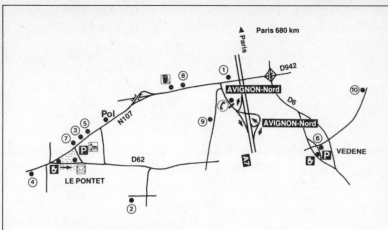

Hotels
- ① **Sofitel** LLL 84700 Sorgues ☎ 90 31 16 43
- ② **Aub. de Cassagne** LL 84130 Le Pontet ☎ 90 31 04 18 F:12,1,Ds(11-3)
- ③ **Christina** (*sans rest*) LL 84130 Le Pontet ☎ 90 31 13 62 F:10-3

Garages
- ④ **Vaucluse-Auto** (Peugeot-Talbot)

Banques
- ⑤ **Caisse d'Epargne** ⑥ **Caisse d'Epargne** ⑦ **Crédit Lyonnais**

S/marché
- ⑧ **Auchan**

Camping
- ⑨ **Le Grand Bois** 84130 Le Pontet ☎ 90 31 37 44 F:12-3
- ⑩ **Flory** 84270 Vedène ☎ 90 31 00 51 F:10-3(mi)

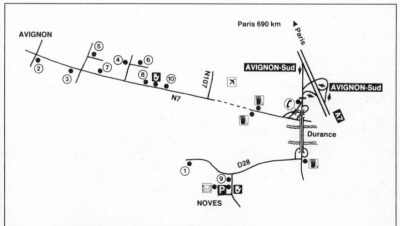

Hotels
- ① **Aub. de Noves** LLL 13550 Noves ☎ 90 94 19 21 F:1,2
- ② **Mercure** LLL 84000 Avignon ☎ 90 88 91 10
- ③ **Novotel** LLL 84000 Avignon ☎ 90 87 62 36
- ④ **Ibis** L 84140 Avignon-Montfavet ☎ 90 87 11 00
- ⑤ **Climat de France** de l'Amandier L 84140 Avignon-Montfavet ☎ 90 88 13 00
- ⑥ **Climat de France** de la Cristole L 84140 Avignon-Montfavet ☎ 90 88 15 00

Garages
- ⑦ **A.S.A.** (Renault) ⑧ **Ste-Comm** (Citroën)

Banques
- ⑨ **Banque Chaix**

S/marché
- ⑩ **Mistral 7**

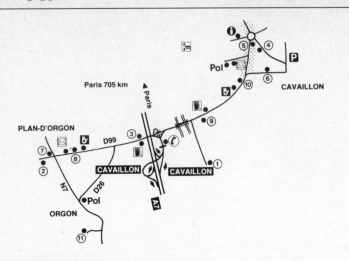

Hotels
① **Christel** LLL 84300 Cavaillon ☎ 90 71 07 79
② **Flamant Rose** L 13750 Plan-d'Orgon ☎ 90 73 10 17
Garages ③ **Manu** (Renault) ④ **Central** (Ford)
Banques ⑤ **BNP** ⑥ **Crédit Agricole** ⑦ **Crédit Agricole** ⑧ **Caisse d'Epargne**
S/marché ⑨ **Intermarché** ⑩ **Montlaur**
Camping ⑪ **La Vallée Heureuse** 13660 Orgon ☎ 90 73 02 78 F:11-3

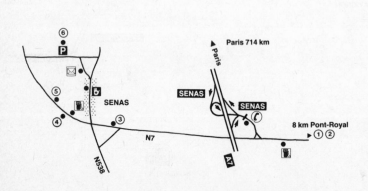

Hotels
① **Moulin de Vernègues** LLLL Pont-Royal, 13370 Mallemort ☎ 90 59 12 00
② **Le Provençal** L Pont Royal, 13370 Mallemort ☎ 90 57 40 64 F:1,6,D
Rests ③ **Lubéron** (*avec ch*) L 13560 Sénas ☎ 90 57 20 10 F:10-12,L(s),Ma
④ **Terminus** (*avec ch*) L 13560 Sénas ☎ 90 57 20 08 F:1,J
Garages ⑤ **Roger Caire** (Ford)
Banques ⑥ **Crédit Agricole**

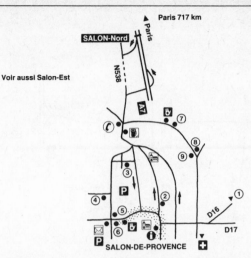

Hotels
① **Abbaye de Ste-Croix** LLL 13300 Salon-de-Provence ☎ 90 56 24 55 F:11(mi)-1
② **Vendôme** (*sans rest*) L 34 r. Mar.-Joffre, 13300 Salon-de-Prov ☎ 90 56 01 96
③ **Sélect** (*sans rest*) L 35 r. Suffren, 13300 Salon-de-Prov ☎ 90 56 07 17
Rests   ④ **Robin** LLL 1 bd. G.-Clemenceau, 13300 Salon-de-Prov ☎ 90 56 06 53 F:2,D(s),L
Banques ⑤ **Banque Chaix** ⑥ **Crédit Lyonnais** ⑦ **Crédit Agricole** ⑧ **Société Générale**
S/marché ⑨ **Sodim**

Hotels
① **Midi** LL 518 allées Craponne, 13300 Salon-de-Prov ☎ 90 53 34 67 F:11,12
② **Roi René** (*sans rest*) LL 561 all. Craponne, 13300 Salon ☎ 90 53 20 22 F:1
③ **Ibis** L 13300 Salon-de-Provence ☎ 90 42 23 57
Garages ④ **S.A.P.A.S.** (Renault) ⑤ **AGM Sarl** (Fiat) ⑥ **Craponne** (Volvo)
Banques ⑦ **Crédit Agricole** ⑧ **Crédit Lyonnais**
S/marché ⑨ **Léclerc** ⑩ **Géant Casino**

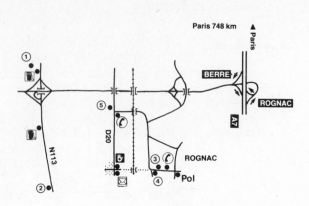

Hotels ① **Cadet Roussel** L 13340 Rognac ☎ 42 87 00 33 F:D
Rests ② **Host. Royal Provence** (*avec ch*) LL 13340 Rognac ☎ 42 87 00 27 F:7,D(s)
Banques ③ **Société Générale** ④ **Caisse d'Epargne**
S/marché ⑤ **Genty Super**

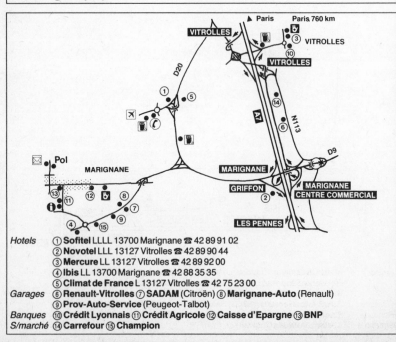

Hotels ① **Sofitel** LLLLL 13700 Marignane ☎ 42 89 91 02
② **Novotel** LLLL 13127 Vitrolles ☎ 42 89 90 44
③ **Mercure** LL 13127 Vitrolles ☎ 42 89 92 00
④ **Ibis** LL 13700 Marignane ☎ 42 88 35 35
⑤ **Climat de France** L 13127 Vitrolles ☎ 42 75 23 00
Garages ⑥ **Renault-Vitrolles** ⑦ **SADAM** (Citroën) ⑧ **Marignane-Auto** (Renault)
⑨ **Prov-Auto-Service** (Peugeot-Talbot)
Banques ⑩ **Crédit Lyonnais** ⑪ **Crédit Agricole** ⑫ **Caisse d'Epargne** ⑬ **BNP**
S/marché ⑭ **Carrefour** ⑮ **Champion**

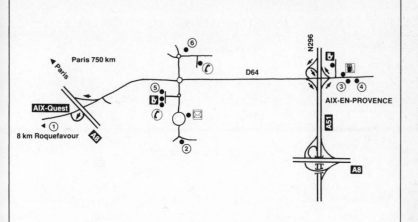

Hotels   ① **Arquier** LL Roquefavour, 13122 Ventabren ☎ 42 24 20 45 F:2,D(s),L
        ② **Campanile** L 13090 Aix-en-Provence ☎ 42 59 40 73
Garages ③ **Verdun-Aix** (Renault) ④ **Galice-Auto** (Peugeot-Talbot)
Banques ⑤ **Crédit Lyonnais**
S/marché ⑥ **Rallyé**

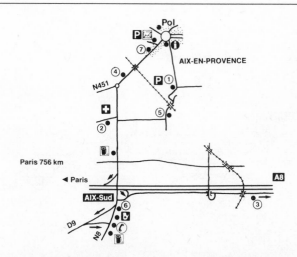

Hotels   ① **Paul Cézanne** (*sans rest*) LLLL 40 av. V.-Hugo, 13100 Aix-en-Provence ☎ 42 26 34 73
        ② **P.L.M. Le Pigonnet** LLL 5 av. Pigonnet, 13100 Aix-en-Prov ☎ 42 59 02 90
        ③ **Novotel Aix Sud** LLL 13100 Aix-en-Provence ☎ 42 27 90 49
        ④ **Rés. Rotonde** (*sans rest*) LL 15 av. Belges, 13100 Aix ☎ 42 26 29 88 F:12,1
        ⑤ **Le Moulin** (*sans rest*) LL 1 av. Schumann, 13090 Aix ☎ 42 59 41 68 F:12,1
Banques ⑥ **Crédit Lyonnais** ⑦ **Crédit du Nord**

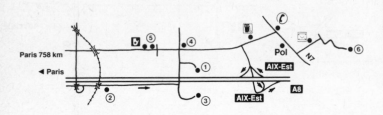

AIX-EN-PROVENCE

Hotels	① **Novotel Aix Est** LLL 13100 Aix-en-Provence ☎ 42 27 47 50
	② **Novotel Aix Sud** LLL 13100 Aix-en-Provence ☎ 42 27 90 49
	③ **Ibis** L 13100 Aix-en-Provence ☎ 42 27 98 20
Banques	④ **Caisse d'Epargne** ⑤ **Crédit Lyonnais**
Camping	⑥ **Chantecler** av. du Val St-André, 13100 Aix-en-Provence ☎ 42 26 12 98

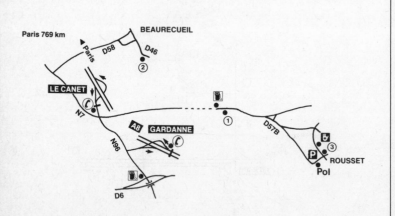

Hotels	① **La Galinière** LL Châteauneuf-le-Rouge, 13790 Rousset ☎ 42 58 62 04
Rests	② **Relais Ste-Victoire** (*avec ch*) LLL Beaurecueil, 13100 Aix ☎ 42 28 94 98
	F:2,11,D(s),L,Ma(10-2)
Banques	③ **Crédit Agricole**

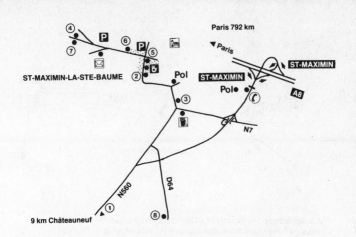

Paris 792 km

ST-MAXIMIN-LA-STE-BAUME

Pol

ST-MAXIMIN

Pol

N7

N560

D64

9 km Châteauneuf

Hotels	① **Châteauneuf** LLL Châteauneuf, 83860 Nans-les-Pins ☎ 94 78 90 06 F:11-3	
Rests	② **Chez Nous** LL 83470 St-Maximin-la-Ste-Baume ☎ 94 78 02 57 F:12-1(mi), Me	
Garages	③ **St-Maximin Auto** (Renault) ④ **Grimaud** (Peugeot-Talbot)	
Banques	⑤ **Société Générale** ⑥ **Crédit Lyonnais**	
S/marché	⑦ **Sodim**	
Camping	⑧ **Provençal** 83470 St-Maximin-la-Ste-Baume ☎ 94 78 16 97 F:10-3	

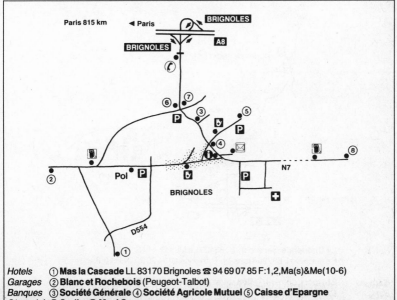

Paris 815 km

BRIGNOLES

BRIGNOLES

A8

Pol

BRIGNOLES

N7

D554

Hotels	① **Mas la Cascade** LL 83170 Brignoles ☎ 94 69 07 85 F:1,2,Ma(s)&Me(10-6)
Garages	② **Blanc et Rochebois** (Peugeot-Talbot)
Banques	③ **Société Générale** ④ **Société Agricole Mutuel** ⑤ **Caisse d'Epargne**
S/marché	⑥ **Sodim** ⑦ **Maxi Coop**
Camping	⑧ **Municipal** 83170 Brignoles ☎ 94 69 20 10 F:9-3(mi)

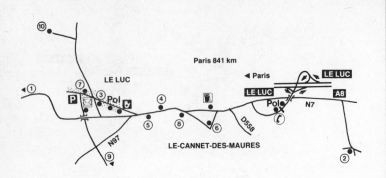

Hotels	① **La Grillade au feu de bois** LL (4 km 0) 83340 Le Luc ☎ 94 69 71 20
	② **Mas du Four** L Le Cannet-des-Maures, 83340 Le Luc ☎ 94 60 74 64 F:1,2,10,D(s)&L(9-6)
Rests	③ **Host. du Parc** (*avec ch*) LL 83340 Le Luc ☎ 94 60 70 01 F:5,11,12,L(s),Ma
Garages	④ **Pelizzaro** (Fiat) ⑤ **Les Oliviers** (Ford)
Banques	⑥ **Crédit Agricole** ⑦ **Crédit Lyonnais**
S/marché	⑧ **Intermarché**
Camping	⑨ **Les Bruyères** 83340 Le Luc ☎ 94 73 47 07
	⑩ **Municipal** 83340 Le Luc ☎ 94 60 80 50 F:9(mi)-5(mi)

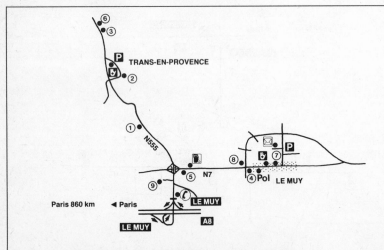

Hotels	① **La Chêneraie** (*sans rest*) L 83490 Le Muy ☎ 94 45 14 43
	② **Commerce** L 83720 Trans-en-Provence ☎ 94 70 80 04 F:10-3,V
	③ **Climat de France** L 83720 Trans-en-Provence ☎ 94 70 82 11
Garages	④ **St-Roch** (Citroën) ⑤ **Bousquet** (Peugeot-Talbot) ⑥ **S.A.V.A.** (Renault)
Banques	⑦ **Caisse d'Epargne**
S/marché	⑧ **Genty**
Camping	⑨ **Les Cigales** 83490 Le Muy ☎ 94 45 12 08 F:9(mi)-6

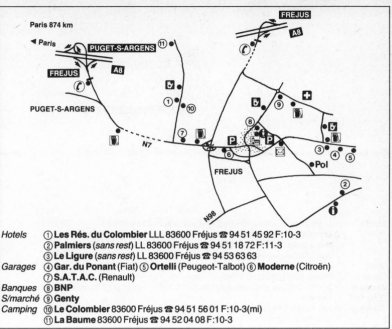

Hotels ① **Les Rés. du Colombier** LLL 83600 Fréjus ☎ 94 51 45 92 F:10-3
② **Palmiers** (*sans rest*) LL 83600 Fréjus ☎ 94 51 18 72 F:11-3
③ **Le Ligure** (*sans rest*) LL 83600 Fréjus ☎ 94 53 63 63
Garages ④ **Gar. du Ponant** (Fiat) ⑤ **Ortelli** (Peugeot-Talbot) ⑥ **Moderne** (Citroën)
⑦ **S.A.T.A.C.** (Renault)
Banques ⑧ **BNP**
S/marché ⑨ **Genty**
Camping ⑩ **Le Colombier** 83600 Fréjus ☎ 94 51 56 01 F:10-3(mi)
⑪ **La Baume** 83600 Fréjus ☎ 94 52 04 08 F:10-3

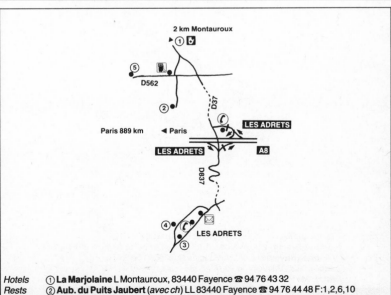

Hotels ① **La Marjolaine** L Montauroux, 83440 Fayence ☎ 94 76 43 32
Rests ② **Aub. du Puits Jaubert** (*avec ch*) LL 83440 Fayence ☎ 94 76 44 48 F:1,2,6,10
③ **Le Logis des Manons** (*avec ch*) L Les Adrets, 83600 Fréjus ☎ 94 40 90 95 F:11,12
Garages ④ **Marras**
S/marché ⑤ **Leclerc**

Hotels
① **Loews** LLLL La Napoule, 06210 Mandelieu ☎ 93 49 90 00
② **Ermitage du Riou** LLL La Napoule, 06210 Mandelieu ☎ 93 49 95 56
③ **Plaza** (*sans rest*) LL 06210 Mandelieu ☎ 93 49 41 03 F:12(mi)-1(mi)
④ **Sant'Angelo** (*sans rest*) L 06210 Mandelieu ☎ 93 49 28 23
⑤ **Climat de France** L 06150 Cannes-La-Bocca ☎ 93 90 22 22
⑥ **Campanile** L 06150 Cannes-La-Bocca ☎ 93 48 69 41
Banques ⑦ **BNP** ⑧ **Caisse d'Epargne** ⑨ **Soc. Gén.** ⑩ **Cr. Agricole** ⑪ **Banque Populaire**
S/marché ⑫ **Rallye**
Camping ⑬ **Les Cigales** 06210 Mandelieu ☎ 93 49 23 53
⑭ **Les Pruniers** 06210 Mandelieu ☎ 93 49 99 23 F:10-3

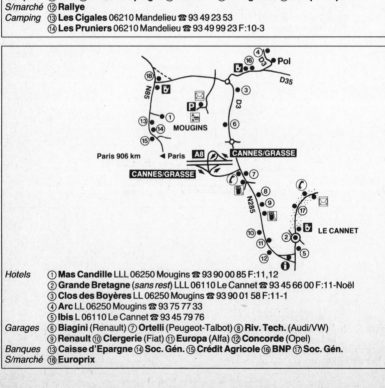

Hotels
① **Mas Candille** LLL 06250 Mougins ☎ 93 90 00 85 F:11,12
② **Grande Bretagne** (*sans rest*) LLL 06110 Le Cannet ☎ 93 45 66 00 F:11-Noël
③ **Clos des Boyères** LL 06250 Mougins ☎ 93 90 01 58 F:11-1
④ **Arc** LL 06250 Mougins ☎ 93 75 77 33
⑤ **Ibis** L 06110 Le Cannet ☎ 93 45 79 76
Garages ⑥ **Biagini** (Renault) ⑦ **Ortelli** (Peugeot-Talbot) ⑧ **Riv. Tech.** (Audi/VW)
⑨ **Renault** ⑩ **Clergerie** (Fiat) ⑪ **Europa** (Alfa) ⑫ **Concorde** (Opel)
Banques ⑬ **Caisse d'Epargne** ⑭ **Soc. Gén.** ⑮ **Crédit Agricole** ⑯ **BNP** ⑰ **Soc. Gén.**
S/marché ⑱ **Europrix**

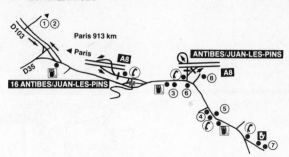

Hotels
- ① **Novotel** LLL Sophia Antipolis, 06560 Valbonne ☎ 93 33 38 00
- ② **Ibis** L Sophia Antipolis, 06560 Valbonne ☎ 93 33 50 60
- ③ **Fimotel** L 06600 Antibes ☎ 93 74 46 36

Garages ④ **Riviera** (Citroën) ⑤ **Charreau-Auto** (Renault) ⑥ **Sport-Auto-Rte.** (Audi/VW)

Banques ⑦ **BNP**

S/marché ⑧ **Carrefour**

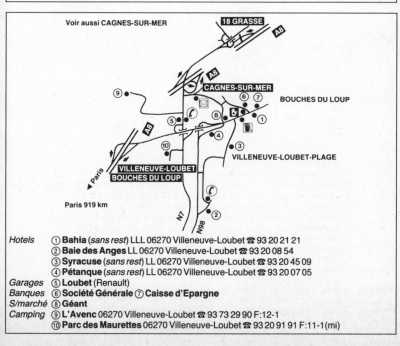

Hotels
- ① **Bahia** (*sans rest*) LLL 06270 Villeneuve-Loubet ☎ 93 20 21 21
- ② **Baie des Anges** LL 06270 Villeneuve-Loubet ☎ 93 20 08 54
- ③ **Syracuse** (*sans rest*) LL 06270 Villeneuve-Loubet ☎ 93 20 45 09
- ④ **Pétanque** (*sans rest*) LL 06270 Villeneuve-Loubet ☎ 93 20 07 05

Garages ⑤ **Loubet** (Renault)

Banques ⑥ **Société Générale** ⑦ **Caisse d'Epargne**

S/marché ⑧ **Géant**

Camping
- ⑨ **L'Avenc** 06270 Villeneuve-Loubet ☎ 93 73 29 90 F:12-1
- ⑩ **Parc des Maurettes** 06270 Villeneuve-Loubet ☎ 93 20 91 91 F:11-1 (mi)

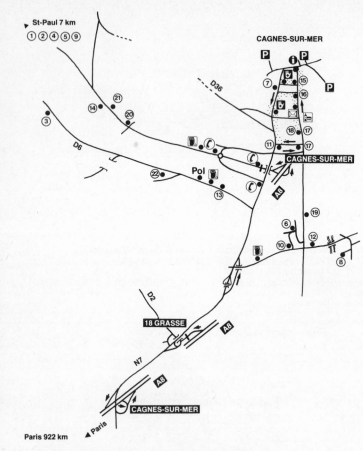

CAGNES-SUR-MER

St-Paul 7 km
① ② ④ ⑤ ⑨

CAGNES-SUR-MER

A8

18 GRASSE

A8

A8

CAGNES-SUR-MER

Paris 922 km

Hotels	
	① **Mas d'Artigny** LLLL 06570 St-Paul ☎ 93 32 84 54
	② **La Colombe d'Or** LLL 06570 St-Paul ☎ 93 32 80 02 F:11-Noël
	③ **Hamotel** (*sans rest*) LLL 06270 Villeneuve-Loubet ☎ 93 20 86 60 F:11-12(mi)
	④ **Le Hameau** (*sans rest*) LL 06570 St-Paul ☎ 93 32 80 24 F:11-1
	⑤ **Orangers** (*sans rest*) LL 06570 St-Paul ☎ 93 32 80 95
	⑥ **Brasilia** (*sans rest*) LL 06800 Cagnes-sur-Mer ☎ 93 20 25 03
	⑦ **Savournin** (*sans rest*) LL 06800 Cagnes-sur-Mer ☎ 93 20 60 58 F:10,11
	⑧ **Val Duchesse** (*sans rest*) LL 06170 Cros-de-Cagnes ☎ 93 20 10 04
	⑨ **Climat de France** L 06570 St-Paul ☎ 93 32 94 24
	⑩ **Le Derby** L 06800 Cagnes-sur-Mer ☎ 93 20 08 57 F:12
Garages	⑪ **Gral Auto** (Fiat) ⑫ **Stade** (Opel) ⑬ **Mondial** (Renault)
	⑭ **Ortelli** (Peugeot-Talbot)
Banques	⑮ **BNP** ⑯ **Crédit Lyonnais** ⑰ **Société Générale** ⑱ **Caisse d'Epargne** ⑲ **Barclays**
S/marché	⑳ **Genty**
Camping	㉑ **Parc St-Jean** 06800 Cagnes-sur-Mer ☎ 93 20 15 66 F:10-4
	㉒ **L'Oasis** 06800 Cagnes-sur-Mer ☎ 93 20 75 67 F:10(mi)-1

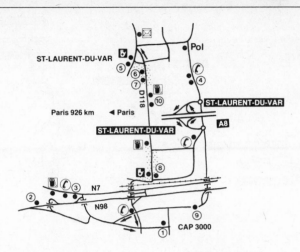

Hotels
① **Novotel** LLL Cap 3000, 06700 St-Laurent-du-Var ☎ 93 31 61 15
② **Motel Delta 21** (*sans rest*) LL 06700 St-Laurent-du-Var ☎ 93 31 75 60 F:11-3
③ **Le Gabian** (*sans rest*) L 06700 St-Laurent-du-Var ☎ 93 31 24 95 F:11,12
Garages ④ **Pesage 2000** (Lancia)
Banques ⑤ **Banque Populaire** ⑥ **Caisse d'Epargne** ⑦ **BNP** ⑧ **Crédit Agricole**
S/marché ⑨ **Super 3000** ⑩ **Intermarché**

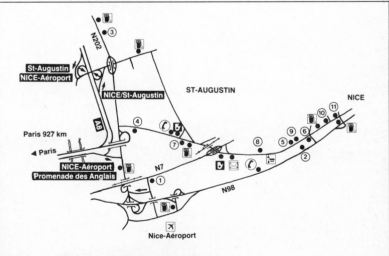

Hotels
① **Holiday Inn** LLL 06200 Nice ☎ 93 83 91 92
② **Ibis** L 06200 Nice ☎ 93 83 30 30
③ **Climat de France** L 06200 Nice ☎ 93 71 80 80
Garages ④ **Gds. Gar. Nice** (Peugeot-Talbot) ⑤ **Succursale** (Citroën) ⑥ **Gral** (Fiat)
Banques ⑦ **Crédit Lyonnais** ⑧ **Crédit Agricole** ⑨ **Société Générale** ⑩ **BNP**
S/marché ⑪ **Casino**

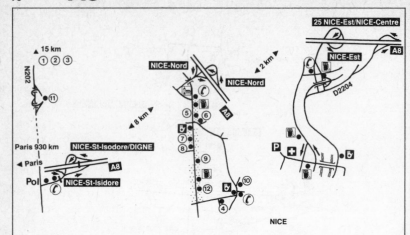

Hotels ① **Servotel** LL 06670 Castagniers-les-Moulins ☎ 93 08 22 00
② **Les Relais Bleus** L 06670 La Roquette/Var ☎ 93 08 42 32
Rests ③ **Issautier** LLL 06670 St-Martin-du-Var ☎ 93 08 10 65 F:2-3(mi),D(s),L
④ **Gourmet Lorrain** (avec ch) LL 06100 Nice ☎ 93 84 90 78 F:8,D(s),L
Banques ⑤ **Crédit Lyonnais** ⑥ **Caisse d'Epargne** ⑦ **Crédit Agricole** ⑧ **Banque Populaire**
⑨ **BNP** ⑩ **Société Générale**
S/marché ⑪ **Carrefour** ⑫ **Prisunic**

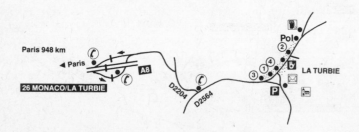

Hotels ① **Le Napoléon** LL La Turbie, 06320 Cap-d'Ail ☎ 93 41 00 54 F:2(mi)-3,Ma(10-3)
② **France** L La Turbie, 06320 Cap-d'Ail ☎ 93 41 09 54 F:11-12(mi)
Banques ③ **Crédit Agricole** ④ **BNP**

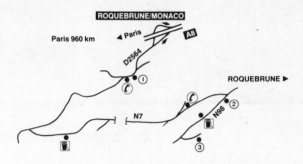

Hotels
① **Vistaëro** LLLL 06190 Roquebrune-Cap-Martin ☎ 93 35 01 50 11-2(mi)
② **Regency** (*sans rest*) L 06190 Roquebrune-Cap-Martin ☎ 93 35 00 91 F:11-Noël
③ **Westminster** L 06190 Roquebrune-Cap-Martin ☎ 93 35 00 68 F:10(mi)-1

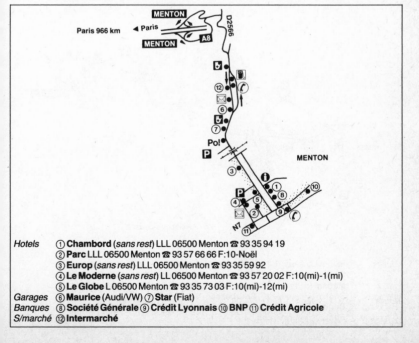

Hotels
① **Chambord** (*sans rest*) LLL 06500 Menton ☎ 93 35 94 19
② **Parc** LLL 06500 Menton ☎ 93 57 66 66 F:10-Noël
③ **Europ** (*sans rest*) LLL 06500 Menton ☎ 93 35 59 92
④ **Le Moderne** (*sans rest*) LL 06500 Menton ☎ 93 57 20 02 F:10(mi)-1(mi)
⑤ **Le Globe** L 06500 Menton ☎ 93 35 73 03 F:10(mi)-12(mi)
Garages ⑥ **Maurice** (Audi/VW) ⑦ **Star** (Fiat)
Banques ⑧ **Société Générale** ⑨ **Crédit Lyonnais** ⑩ **BNP** ⑪ **Crédit Agricole**
S/marché ⑫ **Intermarché**

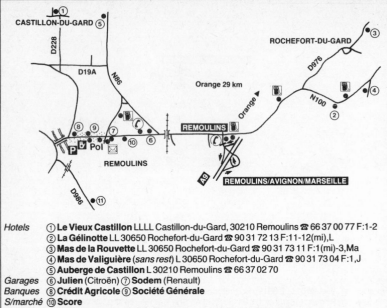

Hotels
  ① **Le Vieux Castillon** LLLL Castillon-du-Gard, 30210 Remoulins ☎ 66 37 00 77 F:1-2
  ② **La Gélinotte** LL 30650 Rochefort-du-Gard ☎ 90 31 72 13 F:11-12(mi),L
  ③ **Mas de la Rouvette** LL 30650 Rochefort-du-Gard ☎ 90 31 73 11 F:1(mi)-3,Ma
  ④ **Mas de Valiguière** (*sans rest*) L 30650 Rochefort-du-Gard ☎ 90 31 73 04 F:1,J
  ⑤ **Auberge de Castillon** L 30210 Remoulins ☎ 66 37 02 70
Garages ⑥ **Julien** (Citroën) ⑦ **Sodem** (Renault)
Banques ⑧ **Crédit Agricole** ⑨ **Société Générale**
S/marché ⑩ **Score**
Camping ⑪ **La Soubeyranne** 30210 Remoulins ☎ 66 37 03 21 F:9(mi)-3

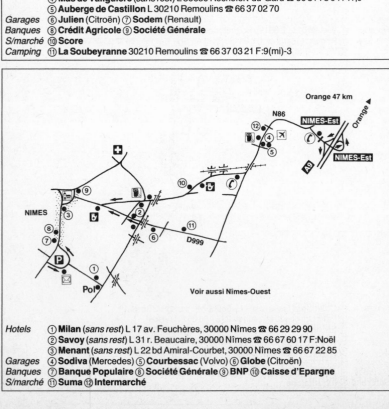

Hotels
  ① **Milan** (*sans rest*) L 17 av. Feuchères, 30000 Nîmes ☎ 66 29 29 90
  ② **Savoy** (*sans rest*) L 31 r. Beaucaire, 30000 Nîmes ☎ 66 67 60 17 F:Noël
  ③ **Menant** (*sans rest*) L 22 bd Amiral-Courbet, 30000 Nîmes ☎ 66 67 22 85
Garages ④ **Sodiva** (Mercedes) ⑤ **Courbessac** (Volvo) ⑥ **Globe** (Citroën)
Banques ⑦ **Banque Populaire** ⑧ **Société Générale** ⑨ **BNP** ⑩ **Caisse d'Epargne**
S/marché ⑪ **Suma** ⑫ **Intermarché**

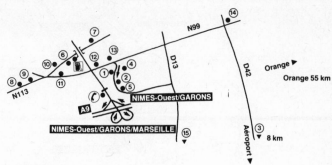

NIMES

N99

N113

A9

NIMES-Ouest/GARONS

NIMES-Ouest/GARONS/MARSEILLE

Orange ▶
Orange 55 km

Aéroport

③ ▼ 8 km

Voir aussi Nîmes-Est

Hotels	① **Novotel** LLL 30000 Nîmes ☎ 66 84 60 20
	② **Mercure** LLL 30000 Nîmes ☎ 66 84 14 55
	③ **Les Aubuns** LLL 30132 Caissargues ☎ 66 70 10 44
	④ **Nimotel** LL 30000 Nîmes ☎ 66 38 13 84
	⑤ **Ibis** L 30000 Nîmes ☎ 66 38 00 65
Garages	⑥ **Gds. Gars. du Gard** (Peugeot-Talbot) ⑦ **Succursale** (Renault) ⑧ **Succursale** (Citroën)
	⑨ **Auto Sport** (Alfa) ⑩ **Europe** (Fiat) ⑪ **du Midi** (Austin-Rover)
Banques	⑫ **Caisse d'Epargne**
S/marché	⑬ **Euromarché** ⑭ **Casino**
Camping	⑮ **Domaine de la Bastide** 30000 Nîmes ☎ 66 38 09 21

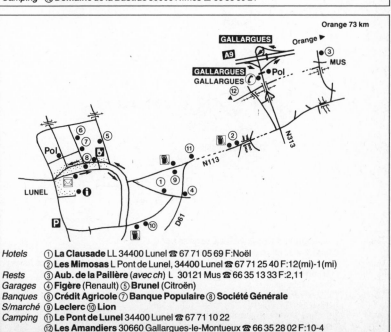

Orange 73 km

GALLARGUES

Orange ▶

A9 ③ MUS

GALLARGUES

GALLARGUES ● Pol

GALLARGUES

⑫

N313

Pol

LUNEL

N113

D61

Hotels	① **La Clausade** LL 34400 Lunel ☎ 67 71 05 69 F:Noël
	② **Les Mimosas** L Pont de Lunel, 34400 Lunel ☎ 67 71 25 40 F:12(mi)-1(mi)
Rests	③ **Aub. de la Paillère** (*avec ch*) L 30121 Mus ☎ 66 35 13 33 F:2,11
Garages	④ **Figère** (Renault) ⑤ **Brunel** (Citroën)
Banques	⑥ **Crédit Agricole** ⑦ **Banque Populaire** ⑧ **Société Générale**
S/marché	⑨ **Leclerc** ⑩ **Lion**
Camping	⑪ **Le Pont de Lunel** 34400 Lunel ☎ 67 71 10 22
	⑫ **Les Amandiers** 30660 Gallargues-le-Montueux ☎ 66 35 28 02 F:10-4

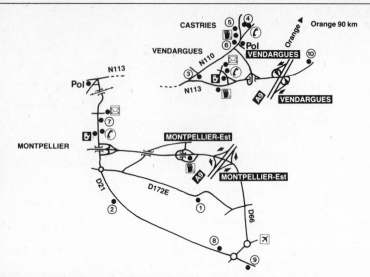

Hotels ① **Demeure des Brousses** LLL 34000 Montpellier ☎ 67 65 77 66 F:10-4
Garages ② **Succursale** (Citroën) ③ **Cano** (Renault)
Banques ④ **Caisse d'Epargne** ⑤ **Crédit Agricole**
S/marché ⑥ **Unico** ⑦ **Suma** ⑧ **Montlaur** ⑨ **Mammouth** ⑩ **Intermarché**

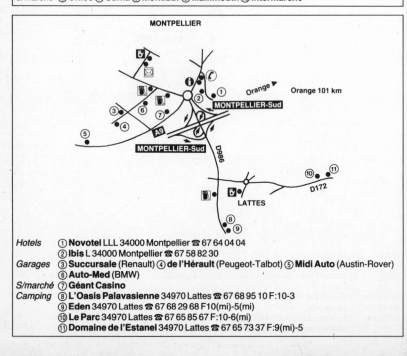

Hotels ① **Novotel** LLL 34000 Montpellier ☎ 67 64 04 04
　　　　② **Ibis** L 34000 Montpellier ☎ 67 58 82 30
Garages ③ **Succursale** (Renault) ④ **de l'Hérault** (Peugeot-Talbot) ⑤ **Midi Auto** (Austin-Rover)
　　　　⑥ **Auto-Med** (BMW)
S/marché ⑦ **Géant Casino**
Camping ⑧ **L'Oasis Palavasienne** 34970 Lattes ☎ 67 68 95 10 F:10-3
　　　　⑨ **Eden** 34970 Lattes ☎ 67 68 29 68 F10(mi)-5(mi)
　　　　⑩ **Le Parc** 34970 Lattes ☎ 67 65 85 67 F:10-6(mi)
　　　　⑪ **Domaine de l'Estanel** 34970 Lattes ☎ 67 65 73 37 F:9(mi)-5

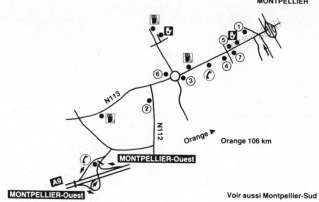

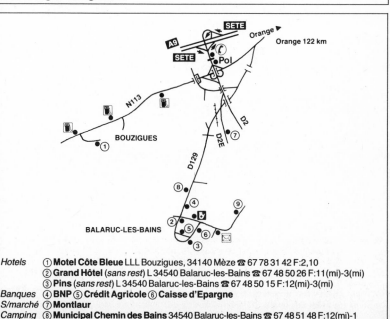

Hotels ① **Myrtes** (*sans rest*) LL 5 av. Lepic, 34100 Montpellier ☎ 67 42 60 11 F:2
Garages ② **Imbert** (Ford) ③ **M.A.S.** (Audi/VW) ④ **Chaptal** (Mercedes)
Banques ⑤ **BNP**
S/marché ⑥ **Leclerc** ⑦ **Casino**

Hotels ① **Motel Côte Bleue** LLL Bouzigues, 34140 Mèze ☎ 67 78 31 42 F:2,10
② **Grand Hôtel** (*sans rest*) L 34540 Balaruc-les-Bains ☎ 67 48 50 26 F:11(mi)-3(mi)
③ **Pins** (*sans rest*) L 34540 Balaruc-les-Bains ☎ 67 48 50 15 F:12(mi)-3(mi)
Banques ④ **BNP** ⑤ **Crédit Agricole** ⑥ **Caisse d'Epargne**
S/marché ⑦ **Montlaur**
Camping ⑧ **Municipal Chemin des Bains** 34540 Balaruc-les-Bains ☎ 67 48 51 48 F:12(mi)-1
⑨ **Municipal Pech d'Ay** 34540 Balaruc-les-Bains ☎ 67 48 50 34 F:12(mi)-2(mi)

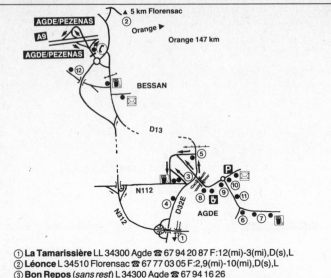

Hotels	① **La Tamarissière** LL 34300 Agde ☎ 67 94 20 87 F:12(mi)-3(mi),D(s),L
	② **Léonce** L 34510 Florensac ☎ 67 77 03 05 F:2,9(mi)-10(mi),D(s),L
	③ **Bon Repos** (*sans rest*) L 34300 Agde ☎ 67 94 16 26
Rests	④ **Aub. de la Grange** (*avec ch*) L 34300 Agde ☎ 67 94 20 66 F:1-3, Ma
Garages	⑤ **Auto-Agde** (Citroën) ⑥ **Dubois** (Renault) ⑦ **Four** (Peugeot-Talbot)
Banques	⑧ **Crédit Lyonnais** ⑨ **Caisse d'Epargne** ⑩ **Crédit Agricole** ⑪ **Banque Populaire**
Camping	⑫ **St-Claude** 34550 Bessan ☎ 67 77 45 66

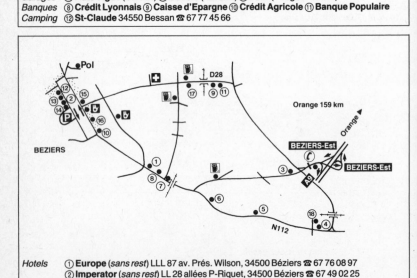

Hotels	① **Europe** (*sans rest*) LLL 87 av. Prés. Wilson, 34500 Béziers ☎ 67 76 08 97
	② **Imperator** (*sans rest*) LL 28 allées P-Riquet, 34500 Béziers ☎ 67 49 02 25
	③ **Ibis** L 34420 Villeneuve-lès-Béziers ☎ 67 62 55 14
Garages	④ **Wilson** (Fiat) ⑤ **Autorama** (BMW) ⑥ **St-Saens** (Audi/VW) ⑦ **Tressol** (Citroën)
	⑧ **Succursale** (Renault) ⑨ **France-Auto** (Opel) ⑩ **Chapat** (Ford)
	⑪ **Gds. Gar. du Bitterrois** (Peugeot-Talbot)
Banques	⑫ **Crédit Lyonnais** ⑬ **Crédit du Nord** ⑭ **BNP** ⑮ **Banque Populaire** ⑯ **Crédit Ag.**
S/marche	⑰ **Mammouth**
Camping	⑱ **La Vendangeuse** 34420 Villeneuve-lès-Béziers ☎ 67 39 62 80

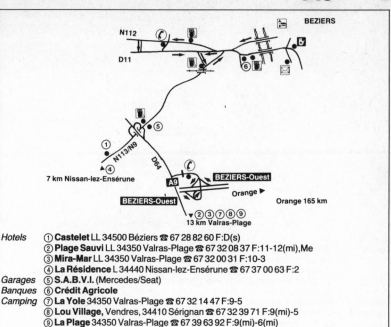

Hotels ① **Castelet** LL 34500 Béziers ☎ 67 28 82 60 F:D(s)
  ② **Plage Sauvi** LL 34350 Valras-Plage ☎ 67 32 08 37 F:11-12(mi),Me
  ③ **Mira-Mar** LL 34350 Valras-Plage ☎ 67 32 00 31 F:10-3
  ④ **La Résidence** L 34440 Nissan-lez-Ensérune ☎ 67 37 00 63 F:2
Garages ⑤ **S.A.B.V.I.** (Mercedes/Seat)
Banques ⑥ **Crédit Agricole**
Camping ⑦ **La Yole** 34350 Valras-Plage ☎ 67 32 14 47 F:9-5
  ⑧ **Lou Village,** Vendres, 34410 Sérignan ☎ 67 32 39 71 F:9(mi)-5
  ⑨ **La Plage** 34350 Valras-Plage ☎ 67 39 63 92 F:9(mi)-6(mi)

Hotels ① **Languedoc** LL 11100 Narbonne ☎ 68 65 14 74
  ② **La Résidence** (sans rest) LL 11100 Narbonne ☎ 68 32 19 41 F:1-2(mi)
  ③ **Midi** LL 11100 Narbonne ☎ 68 41 04 62 F:12(mi)-1(mi),D
  ④ **Regent** (sans rest) L 11100 Narbonne ☎ 68 32 02 41 F:Noël
  ⑤ **Alsace** L 11100 Narbonne ☎ 68 32 01 86
Rests ⑥ **Réverbère** LLL 11100 Narbonne ☎ 68 32 29 18 F:2,D(s),L
Garages ⑦ **Terminus** (Renault)
Banques ⑧ **Banque Populaire** ⑨ **Crédit Lyonnais** ⑩ **BNP** ⑪ **Crédit Agricole**
  ⑫ **Caisse d'Epargne** ⑬ **Société Générale** ⑭ **Crédit Lyonnais**
S/marché ⑮ **Super U** ⑯ **Montlaur**
Camping ⑰ **Le Languedoc** 11100 Narbonne ☎ 68 65 24 65
  ⑱ **Municipal la Falaise** Narbonne-Plage, 11100 Narbonne ☎ 68 49 80 77 F:10-4
  ⑲ **Municipal la Côte des Roses** Narbonne-Plage, 11100 Narbonne ☎ 68 49 83 65

X VOIR AUSSI NARBONNE-EST

Hotels ① **Novotel** LLL 11100 Narbonne ☎ 68 41 59 52
② **Ibis** L 11100 Narbonne ☎ 68 41 14 41
③ **Climat de France** L 11100 Narbonne ☎ 68 41 04 90
Garages ④ **SANDRA** (Renault) ⑤ **Delalieux** (Peugeot-Talbot) ⑥ **Plaisance Auto** (Citroën)
⑦ **Marty** (Audi/VW)
S/marché ⑧ **Mammouth** ⑨ **Casino**
Camping ⑩ **Le Relais de la Nautique** 11100 Narbonne ☎ 68 65 48 19 F:9(mi)-6(mi)
⑪ **Les Mimosas** Mandirac 11100 Narbonne ☎ 68 49 03 72

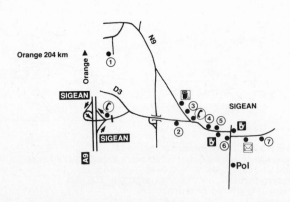

Hotels ① **Château de Villefalse** LL 11130 Sigean ☎ 68 48 21 53 F:11-2,Ma,Me(m)
Garages ② **Roques** (Citroën) ③ **Caccia** (Renault)
Banques ④ **Crédit Lyonnais** ⑤ **Caisse d'Epargne** ⑥ **Crédit Agricole**
S/marché ⑦ **Cordial**

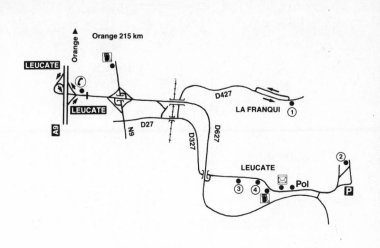

Hotels ① **Plage** L La Franqui, 11370 Leucate ☎ 68 45 70 23 F:10-4
Rests ② **Jouve** (*avec ch*) LL 11370 Leucate ☎ 68 40 02 77 F:10(mi)-3(mi)
Banques ③ **Caisse d'Epargne** ④ **Crédit Agricole**

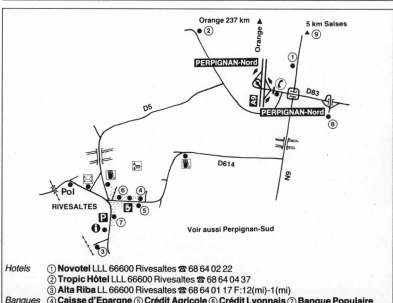

Hotels ① **Novotel** LLL 66600 Rivesaltes ☎ 68 64 02 22
② **Tropic Hôtel** LLL 66600 Rivesaltes ☎ 68 64 04 37
③ **Alta Riba** LL 66600 Rivesaltes ☎ 68 64 01 17 F:12(mi)-1(mi)
Banques ④ **Caisse d'Epargne** ⑤ **Crédit Agricole** ⑥ **Crédit Lyonnais** ⑦ **Banque Populaire**
S/marché ⑧ **Euromarché**
Camping ⑨ **Int. du Roussillon** Salses, 66600 Rivesaltes ☎ 68 38 60 72

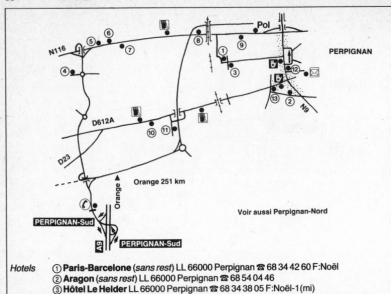

Voir aussi Perpignan-Nord

Hotels	① **Paris-Barcelone** (*sans rest*) LL 66000 Perpignan ☎ 68 34 42 60 F:Noël
	② **Aragon** (*sans rest*) LL 66000 Perpignan ☎ 68 54 04 46
	③ **Hôtel Le Helder** LL 66000 Perpignan ☎ 68 34 38 05 F:Noël-1(mi)
Garages	④ **Fabre** (Volvo) ⑤ **Perpignan Auto** (Fiat) ⑥ **Nord Auto** (Saab) ⑦ **Auto 66** (Opel)
	⑧ **Corbières** (Lancia) ⑨ **Alart** (BMW) ⑩ **Aulas** (Ford) ⑪ **Europe Auto** (Audi/VW)
Banques	⑫ **Crédit Agricole** ⑬ **Caisse d'Epargne**

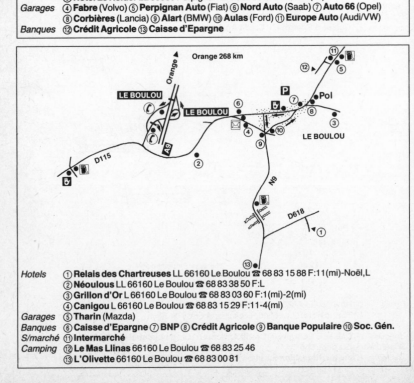

Hotels	① **Relais des Chartreuses** LL 66160 Le Boulou ☎ 68 83 15 88 F:11(mi)-Noël,L
	② **Néoulous** LL 66160 Le Boulou ☎ 68 83 38 50 F:L
	③ **Grillon d'Or** L 66160 Le Boulou ☎ 68 83 03 60 F:1(mi)-2(mi)
	④ **Canigou** L 66160 Le Boulou ☎ 68 83 15 29 F:11-4(mi)
Garages	⑤ **Tharin** (Mazda)
Banques	⑥ **Caisse d'Epargne** ⑦ **BNP** ⑧ **Crédit Agricole** ⑨ **Banque Populaire** ⑩ **Soc. Gén.**
S/marché	⑪ **Intermarché**
Camping	⑫ **Le Mas Llinas** 66160 Le Boulou ☎ 68 83 25 46
	⑬ **L'Olivette** 66160 Le Boulou ☎ 68 83 00 81

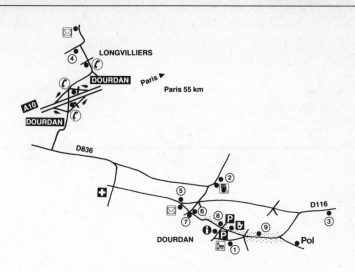

Hotels   ① **Host. Blanche de Castille** LLL 91410 Dourdan ☎ (1) 64 59 68 92
Garages   ② **Côte de Liphard** (Peugeot-Talbot) ③ **Lesage** (Renault) ④ **Leroux** (Renault)
Banques   ⑤ **Banque Populaire** ⑥ **BNP** ⑦ **Société Générale** ⑧ **Crédit Lyonnais**
S/marché ⑨ **Monoprix**

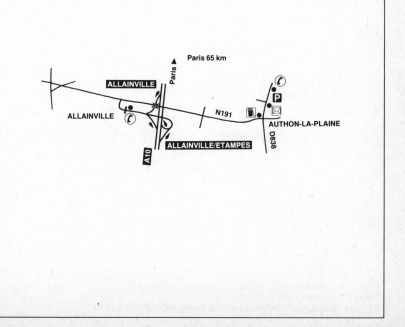

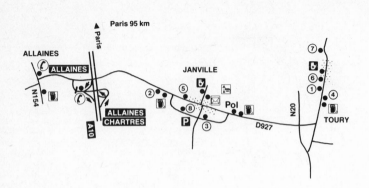

Hotels   ① **Parc** L 28390 Toury ☎ 37 90 50 06 F:2,9,Me
Garages   ② **Denizet** (Citroën) ③ **Godart** (Peugeot-Talbot) ④ **Denizet** (Citroën)
Banques ⑤ **Crédit Agricole** ⑥ **Crédit Lyonnais** ⑦ **Caisse d'Epargne**
S/marché ⑧ **Intermarché**

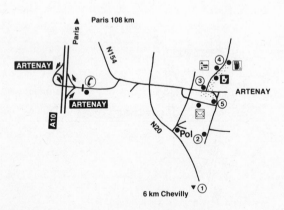

Hotels   ① **Gerbe de Blé** L 45520 Chevilly ☎ 38 80 10 31 F:2,D(s),L
Garages   ② **Sodimavi** (Volvo)
Banques ③ **Société Générale** ④ **Caisse d'Epargne** ⑤ **Crédit Agricole**

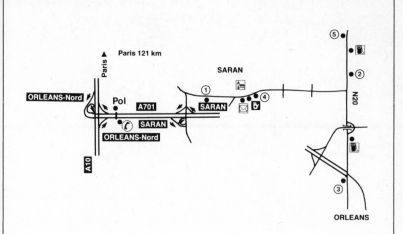

Hotels   ① **Ibis** L 45400 Saran ☎ 38 73 39 93
Garages   ② **France et Delaroche** (Citroën) ③ **Succursale** (Renault)
Banques   ④ **Crédit Agricole**
S/marché ⑤ **Carrefour**

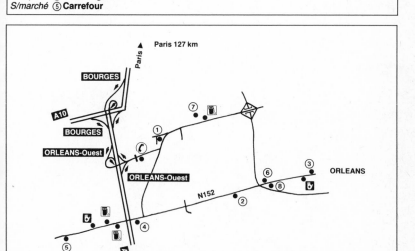

Hotels   ① **Fimotel** L 45380 La Chapelle-St-Mesmin, Orléans ☎ 38 43 71 44
Rests   ② **Aub. de la Montespan** (*avec ch*) LLL 45140 St-Jean-de-la-Ruelle, Orléans
          ☎ 38 88 12 07 F:8, Noël-1
Garages   ③ **Labesse** (BMW) ④ **Gomez** (Audi/VW)
Banques   ⑤ **Crédit Agricole** ⑥ **Société Générale**
S/marché ⑦ **Auchan** ⑧ **Suma**

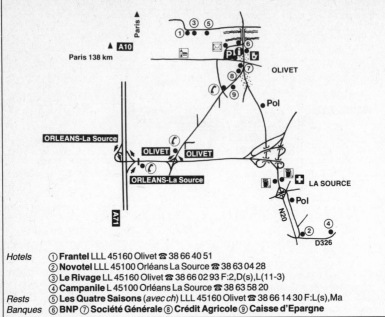

Hotels	
	① **Frantel** LLL 45160 Olivet ☎ 38 66 40 51
	② **Novotel** LLL 45100 Orléans La Source ☎ 38 63 04 28
	③ **Le Rivage** LL 45160 Olivet ☎ 38 66 02 93 F:2,D(s),L(11-3)
	④ **Campanile** L 45100 Orléans La Source ☎ 38 63 58 20
Rests	⑤ **Les Quatre Saisons** (*avec ch*) LLL 45160 Olivet ☎ 38 66 14 30 F:L(s),Ma
Banques	⑥ **BNP** ⑦ **Société Générale** ⑧ **Crédit Agricole** ⑨ **Caisse d'Epargne**

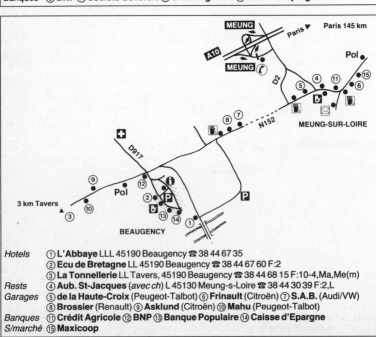

Hotels	
	① **L'Abbaye** LLL 45190 Beaugency ☎ 38 44 67 35
	② **Ecu de Bretagne** LL 45190 Beaugency ☎ 38 44 67 60 F:2
	③ **La Tonnellerie** LL Tavers, 45190 Beaugency ☎ 38 44 68 15 F:10-4,Ma,Me(m)
Rests	④ **Aub. St-Jacques** (*avec ch*) L 45130 Meung-s-Loire ☎ 38 44 30 39 F:2,L
Garages	⑤ **de la Haute-Croix** (Peugeot-Talbot) ⑥ **Frinault** (Citroën) ⑦ **S.A.B.** (Audi/VW)
	⑧ **Brossier** (Renault) ⑨ **Asklund** (Citroën) ⑩ **Mahu** (Peugeot-Talbot)
Banques	⑪ **Crédit Agricole** ⑫ **BNP** ⑬ **Banque Populaire** ⑭ **Caisse d'Epargne**
S/marché	⑮ **Maxicoop**

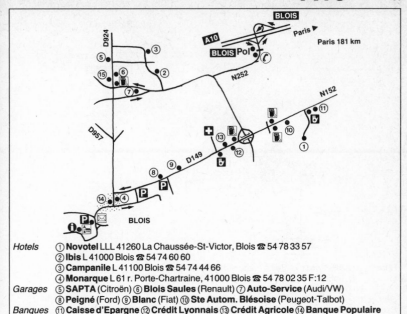

Hotels
① **Novotel** LLL 41260 La Chaussée-St-Victor, Blois ☎ 54 78 33 57
② **Ibis** L 41000 Blois ☎ 54 74 60 60
③ **Campanile** L 41100 Blois ☎ 54 74 44 66
④ **Monarque** L 61 r. Porte-Chartraine, 41000 Blois ☎ 54 78 02 35 F:12

Garages ⑤ **SAPTA** (Citroën) ⑥ **Blois Saules** (Renault) ⑦ **Auto-Service** (Audi/VW)
⑧ **Peigné** (Ford) ⑨ **Blanc** (Fiat) ⑩ **Ste Autom. Blésoise** (Peugeot-Talbot)

Banques ⑪ **Caisse d'Epargne** ⑫ **Crédit Lyonnais** ⑬ **Crédit Agricole** ⑭ **Banque Populaire**

S/marché ⑮ **Leclerc**

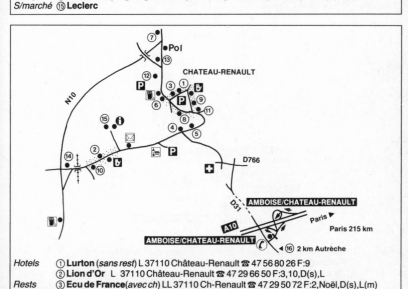

Hotels
① **Lurton** (*sans rest*) L 37110 Château-Renault ☎ 47 56 80 26 F:9
② **Lion d'Or** L 37110 Château-Renault ☎ 47 29 66 50 F:3,10,D(s),L

Rests ③ **Ecu de France** (*avec ch*) LL 37110 Ch-Renault ☎ 47 29 50 72 F:2,Noël,D(s),L(m)

Garages ④ **Thorin** (Renault) ⑤ **du Centre** (Ford) ⑥ **Tortay** (Renault) ⑦ **Gommé** (Citroën)

Banques ⑧ **Crédit Lyonnais** ⑨ **Banque Populaire** ⑩ **Caisse d'Epargne** ⑪ **Crédit Agricole**

S/marché ⑫ **Suma** ⑬ **Radar Maxi** ⑭ **Intermarché**

Camping ⑮ **Municipal du Parc de Vauchevrier** 37110 Ch-Renault ☎ 47 56 54 43 F:10-3
⑯ **Municipal de l'Etang** Autrèche, 37110 Château-Renault F:11-3

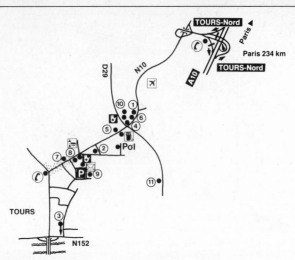

Hotels
① **Ibis Nord** L La Petite Arche 37100 Tours ☎ 47 54 32 20
② **Italia** (*sans rest*) L 19 r. Devilde, 37100 Tours ☎ 47 54 43 01 F:9, Noël
③ **Castel Fleuri** (*sans rest*) L 10 r. Groison, 37100 Tours ☎ 47 54 50 99
Garages ④ **Leu** (Ford) ⑤ **S.E.L.T.A.** (Citroën)
Banques ⑥ **Banque Populaire** ⑦ **Banque Populaire** ⑧ **Société Générale** ⑨ **BNP**
S/marché ⑩ **Mammouth** ⑪ **Suma**

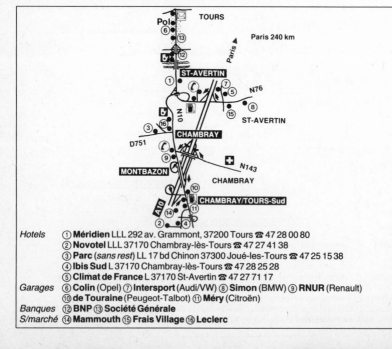

Hotels
① **Méridien** LLL 292 av. Grammont, 37200 Tours ☎ 47 28 00 80
② **Novotel** LLL 37170 Chambray-lès-Tours ☎ 47 27 41 38
③ **Parc** (*sans rest*) LL 17 bd Chinon 37300 Joué-les-Tours ☎ 47 25 15 38
④ **Ibis Sud** L 37170 Chambray-lès-Tours ☎ 47 28 25 28
⑤ **Climat de France** L 37170 St-Avertin ☎ 47 27 71 17
Garages ⑥ **Colin** (Opel) ⑦ **Intersport** (Audi/VW) ⑧ **Simon** (BMW) ⑨ **RNUR** (Renault)
⑩ **de Touraine** (Peugeot-Talbot) ⑪ **Méry** (Citroën)
Banques ⑫ **BNP** ⑬ **Société Générale**
S/marché ⑭ **Mammouth** ⑮ **Frais Village** ⑯ **Leclerc**

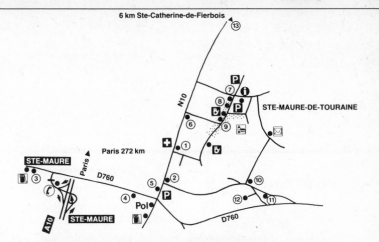

Hotels ① **Veau d'Or** L 37800 Ste-Maure-de-Touraine ☎ 47 65 40 41 F:2,9,10,Ma(s),Me
Rests ② **Gueulardière** (*avec ch*) L 37800 Ste-Maure ☎ 47 65 40 71 F:1,11,D(s),L
Garages ③ **Bou** (Citroën) ④ **Esnault** (Renault) ⑤ **Rico** (Citroën) ⑥ **St-Aubin** (Peugeot-Talbot)
Banques ⑦ **Crédit Lyonnais** ⑧ **Caisse d'Epargne** ⑨ **Banque Populaire**
S/marché ⑩ **Intermarché** ⑪ **Maxicoop**
Camping ⑫ **Municipal de Marans** 37800 Ste-Maure-de-Touraine ☎ 47 65 44 93 F:10-5
⑬ **Parc de Fierbois** Ste-Catherine-de-Fierbois, 37800 Ste-Maure-de-Touraine
☎ 47 65 43 35 F:9-5(mi)

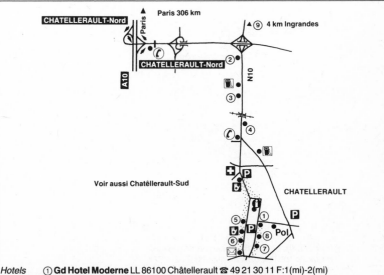

Hotels ① **Gd Hotel Moderne** LL 86100 Châtellerault ☎ 49 21 30 11 F:1(mi)-2(mi)
② **L'Escale** (*sans rest*) L 86100 Châtellerault ☎ 49 21 13 50
Garages ③ **Rousseau** (Peugeot-Talbot) ④ **Eurosport** (Audi/VW)
Banques ⑤ **BNP** ⑥ **Crédit Lyonnais** ⑦ **Crédit Agricole** ⑧ **Banque Populaire**
Camping ⑨ **Le Petit Trianon** Ingrandes, 86220 Dangé-St-Romain ☎ 49 02 61 47 F:10-5(mi)

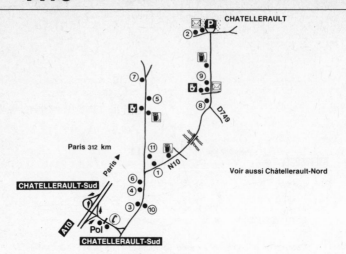

Hotels   ① **Ibis** L 86100 Châtellerault ☎ 49 21 75 77
       ② **Croissant** L 86100 Châtellerault ☎ 49 21 01 77 F:Noël,D(s)
Garages ③ **Raison** (Citroën) ④ **Burban et Lanoue** (Renault) ⑤ **Tardy** (Ford)
       ⑥ **Georget** (Peugeot-Talbot) ⑦ **Robin** (Renault)
Banques ⑧ **Caisse d'Epargne** ⑨ **Crédit Lyonnais**
S/marché ⑩ **Leclerc** ⑪ **Mammouth**

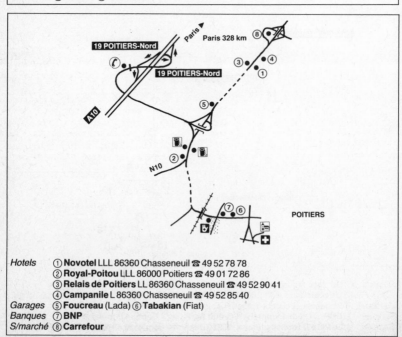

Hotels   ① **Novotel** LLL 86360 Chasseneuil ☎ 49 52 78 78
       ② **Royal-Poitou** LLL 86000 Poitiers ☎ 49 01 72 86
       ③ **Relais de Poitiers** LL 86360 Chasseneuil ☎ 49 52 90 41
       ④ **Campanile** L 86360 Chasseneuil ☎ 49 52 85 40
Garages ⑤ **Foucreau** (Lada) ⑥ **Tabakian** (Fiat)
Banques ⑦ **BNP**
S/marché ⑧ **Carrefour**

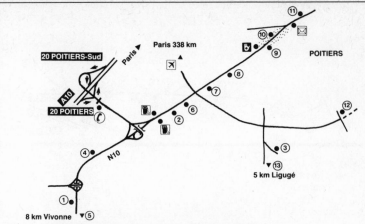

Hotels	① **Bois de la Marche** LLL 86240 Ligugé ☎ 49 53 06 25
	② **Ibis Sud** LL av. du 8 Mai 1945, 86000 Poitiers ☎ 49 53 13 13
Rests	③ **A l'Orée des Bois** (*avec ch*) LL 86280 St-Benoit ☎ 49 57 11 44 F:2,D(s)
	④ **Pierre Benoist** LL 86240 Ligugé ☎ 49 57 11 52 F:2,8,D(s),L
	⑤ **La Treille** (*avec ch*) L 86370 Mouzinne ☎ 49 43 41 13 F:1,2,Me
Garages	⑥ **Diffusion** (Citroën) ⑦ **Centre Auto** (Peugeot-Talbot) ⑧ **Poitou Auto** (Renault)
Banques	⑨ **Crédit Agricole** ⑩ **Crédit Lyonnais** ⑪ **Banque Populaire**
S/marché	⑫ **Intermarché**
Camping	⑬ **Municipal** 86240 Ligugé ☎ 49 55 29 50 F:10-5

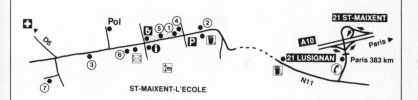

Hotels	① **Cheval Blanc** L 79400 St-Maixent-l'Ecole ☎ 49 05 50 06
Garages	② **Desbrousses** (Citroën) ③ **Mouzin** (Renault)
Banques	④ **Crédit Agricole** ⑤ **BNP** ⑥ **Crédit Lyonnais**
Camping	⑦ **Municipal du Panier Fleuri** 79400 St-Maixent-l'Ecole ☎ 49 05 53 21

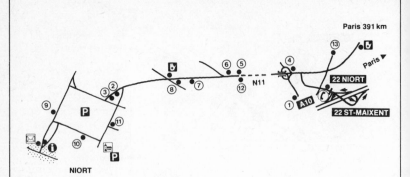

Hotels ① **Motel des Rocs** LLL 79260 La Crèche ☎ 49 25 50 38
② **Grand Hôtel** (*sans rest*) LL 32 av. Paris, 79000 Niort ☎ 49 24 22 21
③ **Paris** (*sans rest*) LL 12 av. Paris, 79000 Niort ☎ 49 24 93 78 F:7, Noël
④ **Campanile** L 79260 La Crèche ☎ 49 25 56 22
Garages ⑤ **Central** (Renault) ⑥ **Deschamps** (Peugeot-Talbot) ⑦ **Béchade** (Citroën)
Banques ⑧ **Caisse d'Epargne** ⑨ **BNP** ⑩ **Banque Populaire** ⑪ **Crédit Agricole**
S/marché ⑫ **Rallyé**
Camping ⑬ **Municipal de Chantoiseau** 79260 La Crèche F:9-6

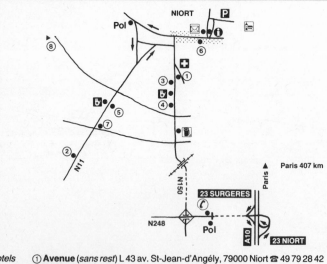

Hotels ① **Avenue** (*sans rest*) L 43 av. St-Jean-d'Angély, 79000 Niort ☎ 49 79 28 42
② **Ibis** L av. de la Rochelle, 79000 Niort ☎ 49 73 54 54
Garages ③ **Succursale** (Citroën)
Banques ④ **BNP** ⑤ **Crédit Agricole** ⑥ **Caisse d'Epargne**
S/marché ⑦ **Intermarché**
Camping ⑧ **Municipal de Noron** 79000 Niort ☎ 49 79 05 33

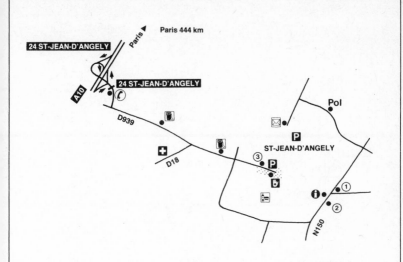

Hotels ① **Paix** L 5 av. Gén.-de-Gaulle, 17400 St-Jean-d'Angély ☎ 46 32 00 93 F:11(mi)-2
Garages ② **Central** (Fiat)
Banques ③ **Société Générale**

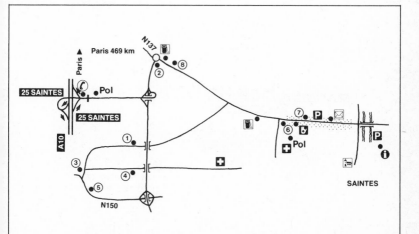

Hotels ① **Relais du Bois St-Georges** LLL r. Royan, 17100 Saintes ☎ 46 93 50 99
 ② **Les Bosquets** LL rte Rochefort, 17100 Saintes ☎ 46 74 04 47 F:Noël
 ③ **Ibis** L rte de Royan, 17100 Saintes ☎ 46 74 36 34
Garages ④ **Bagonneau** (Renault) ⑤ **Guerry** (Peugeot-Talbot)
Banques ⑥ **Banque Populaire** ⑦ **Société Générale**
S/marché ⑧ **Rond point**

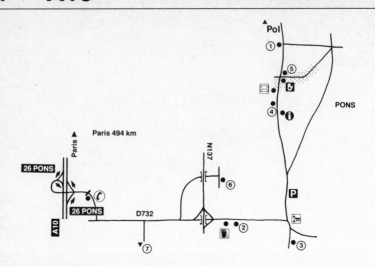

Hotels ① **Auberge Pontoise** LL r. Gambetta, 17800 Pons ☎ 46 94 00 99 F:Noël-1, D(s), L
Garages ② **Colin-Martin** (Citroën) ③ **Marquizeau** (Peugeot-Talbot)
Banques ④ **Crédit Lyonnais** ⑤ **Société Générale**
Camping ⑥ **Municipal** 17800 Pons ☎ 46 91 36 72 F:9(mi)-6
⑦ **Chardon** 17800 Pons ☎ 46 94 04 86 F:12–1

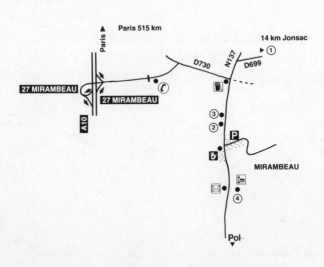

Hotels ① **Le Club** (*sans rest*) L pl. Eglise, 17500 Jonsac ☎ 46 48 02 27
Garages ② **Mirambeau** (Renault)
Banques ③ **Crédit Agricole** ④ **Caisse d'Epargne**

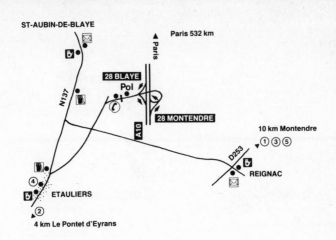

② **Voyageurs** L Le Pontet d'Eyrans, 33390 Blaye ☎ 57 64 71 09 F:10(mi)–11(mi), Me
Garages ③ **Lebrun** (Citroën) Montendre
Banques ④ **Crédit Agricole**
Camping ⑤ **Municipal la Forêt** 17130 Montendre ☎ 46 49 20 17 F:10–4

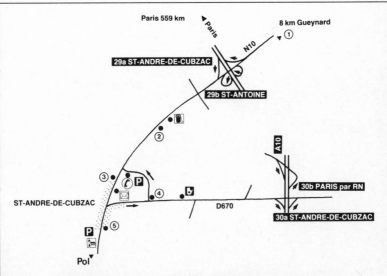

Hotels ① **Le Girondin** (*avec ch*) L Gueynard, 33240 St-André-de-Cubzac ☎ 57 68 71 32
F:Noël-1, Ma(s), Me
Garages ② **B. Cluzeau** (Peugeot-Talbot) ③ **Garage de l'Europe** (Ford)
Banques ④ **Crédit Agricole** ⑤ **Caisse d'Epargne**

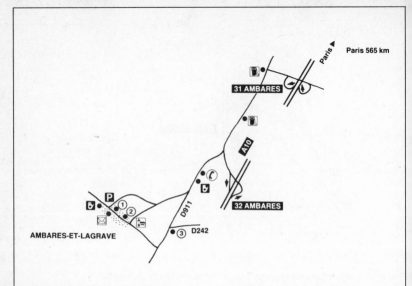

Banques ① **BNP** ② **Caisse d'Epargne**
Camping ③ **Clos Chauvet** 33440 Ambarès-et-Lagrave ☎ 56 38 81 08 F:10(mi)–5(mi)

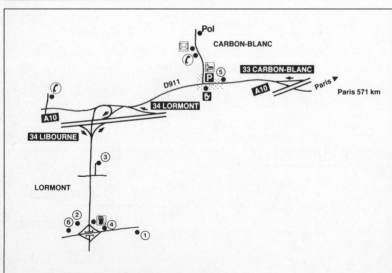

Hotels ① **Campanile** L 33370 Artigues ☎ 56 32 73 32
② **Climat de France** L 33310 Lormont ☎ 56 32 96 10
Garages ③ **Garage de la Ramada** (Renault) ④ **Succursale** (Citroën)
Banques ⑤ **Caisse d'Epargne**
S/marché ⑥ **Rond point**

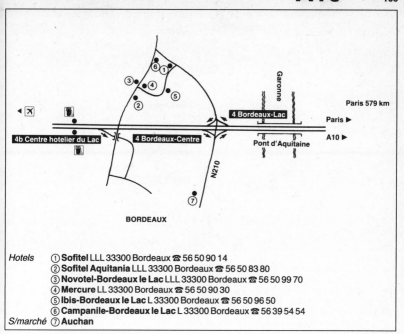

Hotels
① **Sofitel** LLL 33300 Bordeaux ☎ 56 50 90 14
② **Sofitel Aquitania** LLL 33300 Bordeaux ☎ 56 50 83 80
③ **Novotel-Bordeaux le Lac** LLL 33300 Bordeaux ☎ 56 50 99 70
④ **Mercure** LL 33300 Bordeaux ☎ 56 50 90 30
⑤ **Ibis-Bordeaux le Lac** L 33300 Bordeaux ☎ 56 50 96 50
⑥ **Campanile-Bordeaux le Lac** L 33300 Bordeaux ☎ 56 39 54 54
S/marché ⑦ **Auchan**

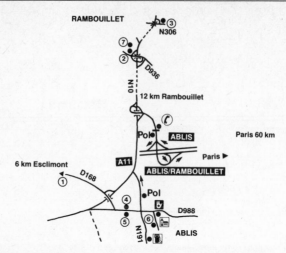

Hotels
- ① **Chateau d'Esclimont** LLLL Esclimont, 28700 Auneau ☎ 37 31 15 15
- ② **Ibis** L Rte Nationale 10, 78120 Rambouillet ☎ (1) 30 41 78 50
- ③ **Climat de France** L Rte Nationale 10, 78120 Rambouillet ☎ (1) 34 85 62 62

Garages
- ④ **Ablis Autos** (Renault)

Banques
- ⑤ **Caisse d'Epargne** ⑥ **Crédit Agricole**

S/marché
- ⑦ **Carrefour** (Rte Nationale 10, Rambouillet)

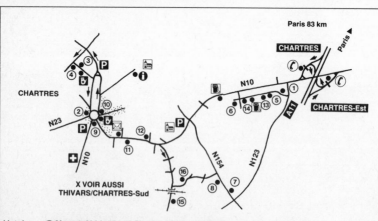

Hotels
- ① **Novotel** LLL 28630 Chartres ☎ 37 34 80 30
- ② **Grand Monarque** LLL 22 pl. Epars, 28000 Chartres ☎ 37 21 00 72
- ③ **Mercure** (*sans rest*) LLL 8 av. Jehan-de-Beauce, 28000 Chartres ☎ 37 21 78 00
- ④ **Jehan de Beauce** (*sans rest*) L 19 av. Jehan-de-Beauce, 28000 Chartres
  ☎ 37 21 01 41 F:12(mi)-1(mi)

Garages
- ⑤ **Chartrains** (Renault) ⑥ **S.E.R.A.C.** (Citroën) ⑦ **Gar. St-Thomas** (Peugeot-Talbot)
- ⑧ **Gar. Electricauto** (Audi/VW)

Banques
- ⑨ **BNP** ⑩ **Crédit Lyonnais** ⑪ **Caisse d'Epargne** ⑫ **Crédit Agricole** ⑬ **Créd. Ag.**

S/marché
- ⑭ **Carrefour** ⑮ **Intermarché**

Camping
- ⑯ **Mun. des Bords de l'Eure** 28000 Chartres ☎ 37 28 79 43 F:11-2

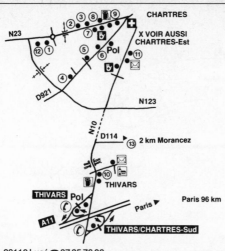

CHARTRES

X VOIR AUSSI CHARTRES-Est

2 km Morancez

THIVARS

Paris 96 km

Hotels ① **Ibis** L 28110 Lucé ☎ 37 35 76 00
Garages ② **Desveaux** (Renault) ③ **Cogedi Auto** (Mercedes) ④ **Socalu** (Toyota)
⑤ **Gar. St-Thomas** (Peugeot-Talbot) ⑥ **Chartres Auto-Sport** (Austin-Rover)
Banques ⑦ **Crédit Lyonnais** ⑧ **Société Générale** ⑨ **Banque Populaire** ⑩ **Crédit Mutuel**
⑪ **Caisse d'Epargne**
S/marché ⑫ **Rallye**
Camping ⑬ **Municipal** Morancez, 28630 Chartres F:10-4

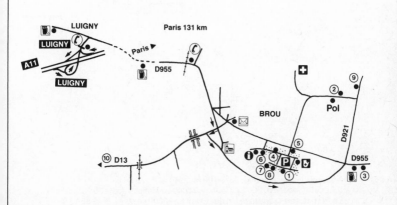

LUIGNY

Paris 131 km

BROU

Hotels ① **Plat d'Etain** L 28160 Brou ☎ 37 47 03 98 F:12(mi)-1(mi)
Garages ② **Royer** (Ren.) ③ **Philippe** (Ren.) ④ **Auguste** (Citroën) ⑤ **Henry** (Peug.-Talb.)
Banques ⑥ **Crédit Agricole** ⑦ **Société Générale** ⑧ **Banque Populaire**
S/marché ⑨ **Intermarché**
Camping ⑩ **Base de Plein Air et de Loisirs** 28160 Brou ☎ 37 47 02 17 F:11-3

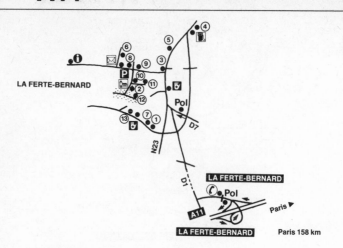

Hotels
① **Climat de France** L 72400 La Ferté-Bernard ☎ 43 93 84 70
② **St-Jean** (*sans rest*) L 72400 La Ferté-Bernard ☎ 43 93 12 83
Rests
③ **Perdrix** (*avec ch*) L 72400 La Ferté-Bernard ☎ 43 93 00 44 F:Ma
Garages
④ **Gd Gar. Fertois** (Renault) ⑤ **Gar. Val d'Huisne** (Peugeot-Talbot) ⑥ **Brion** (Citroën)
⑦ **Gar. de la Rocade** (Peugeot-Talbot)
Banques
⑧ **Caisse d'Epargne** ⑨ **Société Générale** ⑩ **BNP** ⑪ **Crédit Agricole** ⑫ **Crédit Mutuel**
S/marché
⑬ **Leclerc**

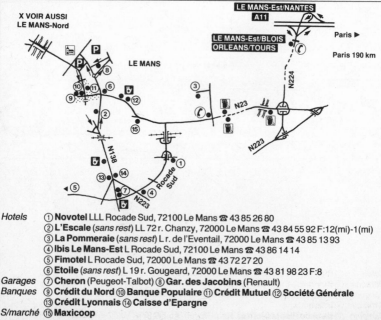

Hotels
① **Novotel** LLL Rocade Sud, 72100 Le Mans ☎ 43 85 26 80
② **L'Escale** (*sans rest*) LL 72 r. Chanzy, 72000 Le Mans ☎ 43 84 55 92 F:12(mi)-1(mi)
③ **La Pommeraie** (*sans rest*) L r. de l'Eventail, 72000 Le Mans ☎ 43 85 13 93
④ **Ibis Le Mans-Est** L Rocade Sud, 72100 Le Mans ☎ 43 86 14 14
⑤ **Fimotel** L Rocade Sud, 72000 Le Mans ☎ 43 72 27 20
⑥ **Etoile** (*sans rest*) L 19 r. Gougeard, 72000 Le Mans ☎ 43 81 98 23 F:8
Garages
⑦ **Cheron** (Peugeot-Talbot) ⑧ **Gar. des Jacobins** (Renault)
Banques
⑨ **Crédit du Nord** ⑩ **Banque Populaire** ⑪ **Crédit Mutuel** ⑫ **Société Générale**
⑬ **Crédit Lyonnais** ⑭ **Caisse d'Epargne**
S/marché
⑮ **Maxicoop**

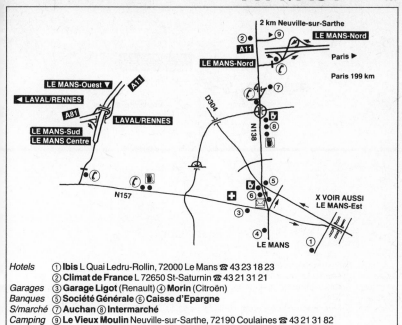

Hotels   ① **Ibis** L Quai Ledru-Rollin, 72000 Le Mans ☎ 43 23 18 23
          ② **Climat de France** L 72650 St-Saturnin ☎ 43 21 31 21
Garages   ③ **Garage Ligot** (Renault) ④ **Morin** (Citroën)
Banques   ⑤ **Société Générale** ⑥ **Caisse d'Epargne**
S/marché   ⑦ **Auchan** ⑧ **Intermarché**
Camping   ⑨ **Le Vieux Moulin** Neuville-sur-Sarthe, 72190 Coulaines ☎ 43 21 31 82

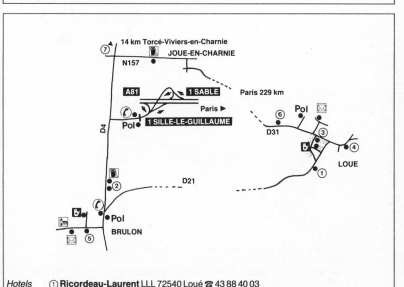

Hotels   ① **Ricordeau-Laurent** LLL 72540 Loué ☎ 43 88 40 03
Garages   ② **Station St-Charles** (Renault)
Banques   ③ **Caisse d'Epargne** ④ **Crédit Agricole** ⑤ **Crédit Mutuel**
S/marché   ⑥ **Unico**
Camping   ⑦ **Municipal de la Charnie** Torcé-Viviers-en-Charnie, 53270 Ste-Suzanne F;10-3

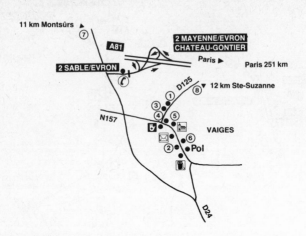

Hotels	① **Commerce** LL 53480 Vaiges ☎ 43 01 20 07 F:2,10,D(s),L
Garages	② **Gar. de la Charnie** (Citroën)
Banques	③ **Crédit Mutuel** ④ **Crédit Agricole** ⑤ **Caisse d'Epargne**
S/marché	⑥ **Unico**
Camping	⑦ **Municipal de la Jouanne** 53150 Montsûrs F:10(mi)-3
	⑧ **Municipal** 53270 Ste-Suzanne

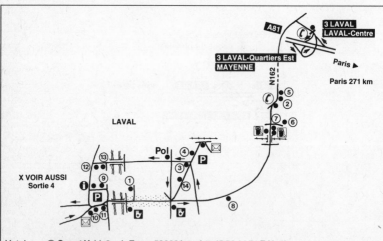

Hotels	① **Ouest H.** LL 3 r. J.-Ferry, 53000 Laval ☎ 43 53 11 71 F:Noël
	② **Ibis** LL 53000 Laval ☎ 43 53 81 82
	③ **Imperial H.** (*sans rest*) LL 61 av. R.-Buron, 53000 Laval ☎ 43 53 55 02 F:8,Noël
	④ **St-Pierre** L 95 av. R.-Buron, 53000 Laval ☎ 43 53 06 10 F:8(mi)-9(mi),Noël,S
Garages	⑤ **Gar. Bassaler** (BMW) ⑥ **Gar. des Touches** (Fiat) ⑦ **Gar. des Pommeraies** (Audi/VW)
	⑧ **Patard** (Mercedes)
Banques	⑨ **Société Générale** ⑩ **Crédit Agricole** ⑪ **Crédit Lyonnais** ⑫ **BNP**
	⑬ **Caisse d'Epargne** ⑭ **Crédit Mutuel**

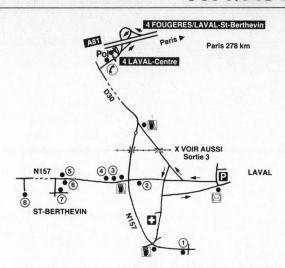

Hotels   ① **Climat de France** L bd des Trappistines (N157), 53000 Laval ☎ 43 49 08 59
Garages   ② **Brilhault** (Citroën) ③ **Gar. des 7 Fontaines** (Opel) ④ **Gar. Chassay** (Alfa/Volvo)
           ⑤ **Hardy** (Renault) ⑥ **Gd Gar. du Maine** (Peugeot-Talbot)
S/marché ⑦ **Leclerc**
Camping   ⑧ **Municipal de Coupeau** 53940 St-Berthevin ☎ 43 69 05 16 F:11-4

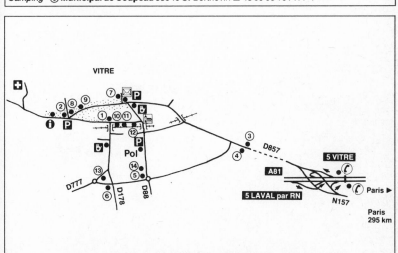

Hotels   ① **Petit-Billot** L 35500 Vitré ☎ 99 75 02 10 F:12(mi)-1(mi),V(s),S
           ② **Chêne Vert** L 35500 Vitré ☎ 99 75 00 58 F:2,9(mi)-10,V(s),S
Garages   ③ **Gar. Pinel** (Citroën) ④ **Vitré Autos** (Renault) ⑤ **Gar. Gendry** (Peugeot-Talbot)
           ⑥ **Mouton** (Audi/VW)
Banques   ⑦ **Crédit Mutuel** ⑧ **BNP** ⑨ **Caisse d'Epargne** ⑩ **Banque Populaire** ⑪ **Crédit Agricole**
           ⑫ **Société Générale**
S/marché ⑬ **Intermarché** ⑭ **Leclerc**

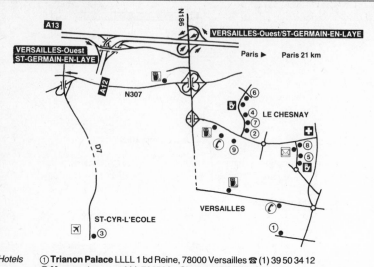

Hotels
① **Trianon Palace** LLLL 1 bd Reine, 78000 Versailles ☎ (1) 39 50 34 12
② **Mercure** (*sans rest*) LL 78150 Le Chesnay ☎ (1) 39 55 11 41
③ **Aérotel** (*sans rest*) LL 88 r. Dr-Vaillant, 78210 St-Cyr-l'Ecole ☎ (1) 30 45 07 44
Garages ④ **Le Chesnay-Auto** (Peugeot-Talbot) ⑤ **Gar. Gymnase** (Renault)
Banques ⑥ **Société Générale** ⑦ **BNP** ⑧ **Crédit Lyonnais**
S/marché ⑨ **Parly 2**

Hotels
① **Novotel** LLL 78630 Orgeval ☎ (1) 39 75 97 60
② **Climat de France** L 78240 Chambourcy ☎ (1) 30 74 42 61
③ **Campanile** L 78100 St-Germain-en-Laye ☎ (1) 34 51 59 59
Rests ④ **Moulin d'Orgeval** (*avec ch*) LL 78630 Orgeval ☎ (1) 39 75 95 74 F:1-2(mi)
Garages ⑤ **Paris-Deauville** (Opel) ⑥ **Lancia** ⑦ **Ouest-Auto** (Citroën)
Banques ⑧ **Caisse d'Epargne** ⑨ **Société Générale**
S/marché ⑩ **Continent**
Camping ⑪ **Les Renardières** 78670 Villennes-sur-Seine ☎ (1) 39 75 88 97

A13

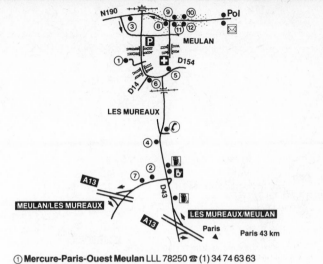

Hotels
1 **Mercure-Paris-Ouest Meulan** LLL 78250 ☎ (1) 34 74 63 63
2 **Climat de France** L 78130 Les Mureaux ☎ (1) 34 74 72 50
Rests
3 **Grande Pinte** (*avec ch*) LL 78250 Meulan ☎ (1) 34 74 15 10 F:2,8,Ma
Garages
4 **Thomas** (Audi/VW) 5 **Mureaux Auto** (Citroën) 6 **Basse-Seine Auto** (Peugeot-Talbot)
7 **G.G.C.** (Ford)
Banques
8 **Crédit Lyonnais** 9 **Caisse d'Epargne** 10 **BNP** 11 **Société Générale** 12 **Crédit Agricole**

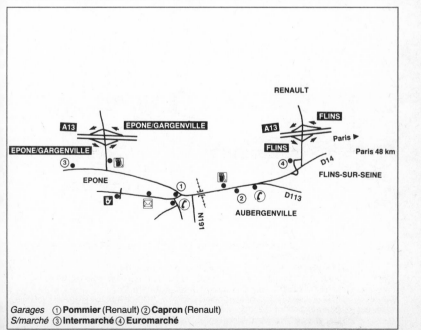

Garages
1 **Pommier** (Renault) 2 **Capron** (Renault)
S/marché
3 **Intermarché** 4 **Euromarché**

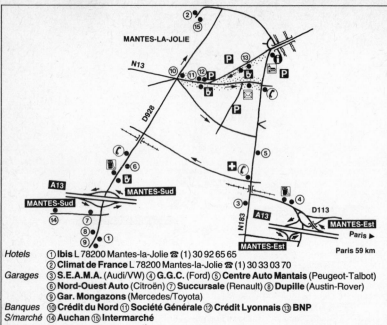

Hotels	① **Ibis** L 78200 Mantes-la-Jolie ☎ (1) 30 92 65 65
	② **Climat de France** L 78200 Mantes-la-Jolie ☎ (1) 30 33 03 70
Garages	③ **S.E.A.M.A.** (Audi/VW) ④ **G.G.C.** (Ford) ⑤ **Centre Auto Mantais** (Peugeot-Talbot)
	⑥ **Nord-Ouest Auto** (Citroën) ⑦ **Succursale** (Renault) ⑧ **Dupille** (Austin-Rover)
	⑨ **Gar. Mongazons** (Mercedes/Toyota)
Banques	⑩ **Crédit du Nord** ⑪ **Société Générale** ⑫ **Crédit Lyonnais** ⑬ **BNP**
S/marché	⑭ **Auchan** ⑮ **Intermarché**

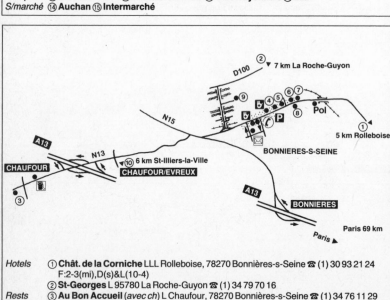

Hotels	① **Chât. de la Corniche** LLL Rolleboise, 78270 Bonnières-s-Seine ☎ (1) 30 93 21 24
	F:2-3(mi),D(s)&L(10-4)
	② **St-Georges** L 95780 La Roche-Guyon ☎ (1) 34 79 70 16
Rests	③ **Au Bon Accueil** (avec ch) L Chaufour, 78270 Bonnières-s-Seine ☎ (1) 34 76 11 29
	F:7(mi)-8(mi),S
Banques	④ **BNP** ⑤ **Caisse d'Epargne** ⑥ **Société Générale** ⑦ **Crédit Agricole** ⑧ **Crédit Lyonnais**
Camping	⑨ **L'Ile aux Loisirs** 78270 Bonnières-s-Seine ☎ (1) 30 93 31 93
	⑩ **La Ferme d'Inchelin** St-Illiers-la-Ville, 78980 Bréval ☎ (1) 34 76 10 11

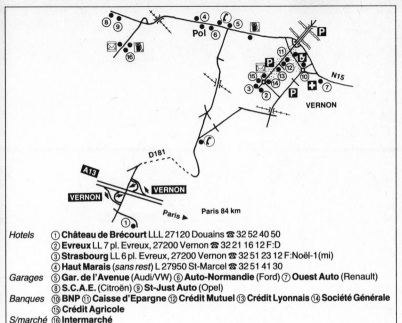

Hotels
① **Château de Brécourt** LLL 27120 Douains ☎ 32 52 40 50
② **Evreux** LL 7 pl. Evreux, 27200 Vernon ☎ 32 21 16 12 F:D
③ **Strasbourg** LL 6 pl. Evreux, 27200 Vernon ☎ 32 51 23 12 F:Noël-1(mi)
④ **Haut Marais** (*sans rest*) L 27950 St-Marcel ☎ 32 51 41 30

Garages ⑤ **Gar. de l'Avenue** (Audi/VW) ⑥ **Auto-Normandie** (Ford) ⑦ **Ouest Auto** (Renault)
⑧ **S.C.A.E.** (Citroën) ⑨ **St-Just Auto** (Opel)

Banques ⑩ **BNP** ⑪ **Caisse d'Epargne** ⑫ **Crédit Mutuel** ⑬ **Crédit Lyonnais** ⑭ **Société Générale**
⑮ **Crédit Agricole**

S/marché ⑯ **Intermarché**

Rests
① **Chaîne d'Or** (*avec ch*) LL 27700 Les Andelys ☎ 32 54 00 31 F:1,D(s)(10-3),L
② **Normandie** (*avec ch*) L 27700 Les Andelys ☎ 32 54 10 52 F:12,Me(s),J

Garages ③ **Renault**

Banques ④ **Crédit Agricole** ⑤ **Société Générale** ⑥ **BNP** ⑦ **Caisse d'Epargne** ⑧ **Crédit Lyonnais**

S/marché ⑨ **Suma** ⑩ **Intermarché**

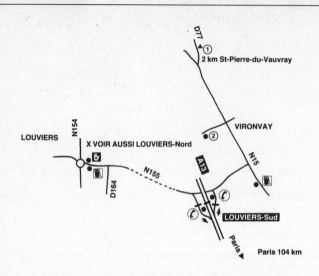

① **Host. St-Pierre** LLL 27430 St-Pierre-du-Vauvray ☎ 32 59 93 29 F:1,2
② **Les Saisons** LL Vironvay, 27400 Louviers ☎ 32 40 02 56 F:2,8

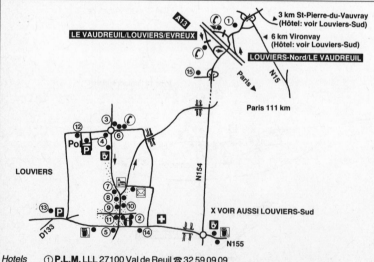

Hotels　① **P.L.M.** LLL 27100 Val de Reuil ☎ 32 59 09 09
　　　　② **Host. de la Poste** L 11 r. Quatre-Moulins, 27400 Louviers ☎ 32 40 01 76
Garages　③ **Cambour-Auto** (Citroën) ④ **Duchemin** (Renault) ⑤ **Dubreuil** (Peugeot-Talbot)
Banques　⑥ **Caisse d'Epargne** ⑦ **Société Générale** ⑧ **Crédit du Nord** ⑨ **Banque Populaire**
　　　　⑩ **BNP** ⑪ **Crédit Lyonnais** ⑫ **Crédit Agricole**
S/marché　⑬ **Champion** ⑭ **Intermarché** ⑮ **Leclerc**

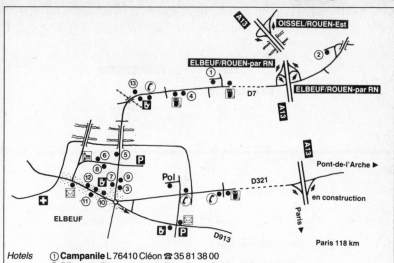

Hotels
- ① **Campanile** L 76410 Cléon ☎ 35 81 38 00
- ② **Climat de France** L 76410 Tourville-la-Rivière ☎ 35 78 49 48
- ③ **Nouvel H.** (*sans rest*) L 43 r. J-Jaurès, 76500 Elbeuf ☎ 35 81 01 02 F:5,8

Garages
- ④ **Gar. du Cours Carnot** (Audi/VW) ⑤ **SECA** (Peugeot-Talbot) ⑥ **S.E.M.V.A.** (Citroën)
- ⑦ **Scemama** (Renault)

Banques
- ⑧ **Soc. Générale** ⑨ **BNP** ⑩ **Caisse d'Epargne** ⑪ **Créd. Lyonnais** ⑫ **Créd. Agricole**

S/marché
- ⑬ **Lion**

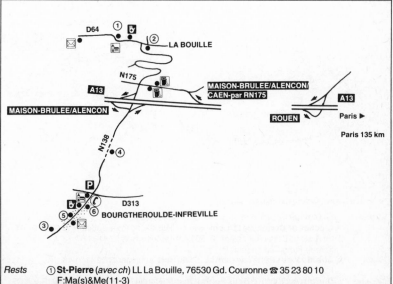

Rests
- ① **St-Pierre** (*avec ch*) LL La Bouille, 76530 Gd. Couronne ☎ 35 23 80 10 F:Ma(s)&Me(11-3)

Garages
- ② **Belloncle** (Renault) ③ **Gar. de la Pépinière** (Peugeot-Talbot)
- ④ **Gar. Vittecoq** (Audi/VW)

Banques
- ⑤ **Crédit Agricole** ⑥ **Caisse d'Epargne**

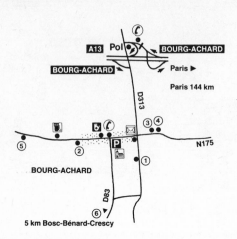

Garages ① **Quilan** (Peugeot-Talbot)
Banques ② **Crédit Agricole** ③ **Caisse d'Epargne** ④ **BNP**
Camping ⑤ **Le Clos Normand** 27310 Bourg-Achard ☎ 32 56 34 84 F:10-3
⑥ **Le Vanneau** Bosc-Bénard-Crescy, 27310 Bourg-Achard ☎ 32 56 42 93 F:10-3

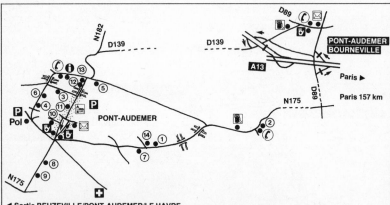

◄ **Sortie BEUZEVILLE/PONT-AUDEMER/LE HAVRE**

Hotels ① **Le Drakkar** LL 27500 Pont-Audemer ☎ 32 41 28 00
② **Cloches de Corneville** LL Corneville-s-Risle, 27500 Pont-Audemer ☎ 32 57 01 04
③ **La Risle** L 16 quai R.-Leblanc, 27500 Pont-Audemer ☎ 32 41 14 57
F:8(mi)-9(mi),12(mi)-1(mi),D
Rests ④ **Aub. du Vieux Puits** (avec ch) LL 27500 Pont-Audemer ☎ 32 41 01 48
F:7,12(mi)-1(mi),L(s),Ma
Garages ⑤ **Durfort** (Audi/VW) ⑥ **Deux Ponts** (Opel) ⑦ **Roulin** (Citroën) ⑧ **Fouquet** (Renault)
⑨ **Ets Delamare** (Peugeot-Talbot)
Banques ⑩ **Crédit Agricole** ⑪ **Crédit Lyonnais** ⑫ **BNP** ⑬ **Crédit Mutuel**
S/marché ⑭ **Lion**

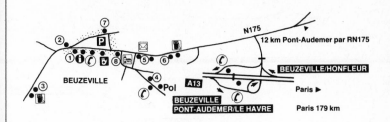

Hotels   ① **Petit Castel** (*sans rest*) LL 27210 Beuzeville ☎ 32 57 76 08 F:12(mi)-1(mi)
Rests   ② **Aub. Cochon d'Or** (*avec ch*) L 27210 Beuzeville ☎ 32 57 70 46 F:12(mi)-1(mi),L
Garages   ③ **Lambert** (Fiat) ④ **Gar. Normandy** (Peugeot-Talbot) ⑤ **Perrin** (Citroën)
          ⑥ **Coquerel** (Renault)
Banques   ⑦ **Crédit Agricole** ⑧ **Caisse d'Epargne**

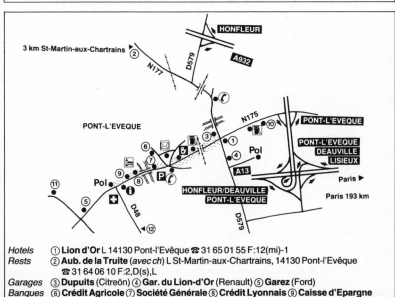

Hotels   ① **Lion d'Or** L 14130 Pont-l'Evêque ☎ 31 65 01 55 F:12(mi)-1
Rests   ② **Aub. de la Truite** (*avec ch*) L St-Martin-aux-Chartrains, 14130 Pont-l'Evêque
          ☎ 31 64 06 10 F:2,D(s),L
Garages   ③ **Dupuits** (Citreön) ④ **Gar. du Lion-d'Or** (Renault) ⑤ **Garez** (Ford)
Banques   ⑥ **Crédit Agricole** ⑦ **Société Générale** ⑧ **Crédit Lyonnais** ⑨ **Caisse d'Epargne**
S/marché ⑩ **Intermarché**
Camping   ⑪ **Municipal** 14130 Pont-l'Evêque ☎ 31 64 15 03 F:10-3
          ⑫ **La Cour de France** 14130 Pont-l'Evêque ☎ 31 64 17 38 F:11-2

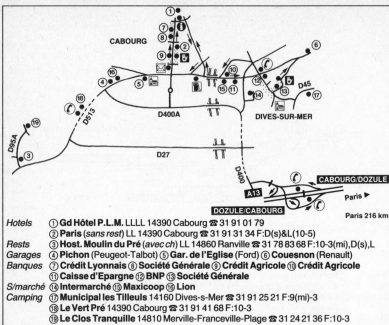

Hotels	① **Gd Hôtel P.L.M.** LLLL 14390 Cabourg ☎ 31 91 01 79
	② **Paris** (*sans rest*) LL 14390 Cabourg ☎ 31 91 31 34 F:D(s)&L(10-5)
Rests	③ **Host. Moulin du Pré** (*avec ch*) LL 14860 Ranville ☎ 31 78 83 68 F:10-3(mi),D(s),L
Garages	④ **Pichon** (Peugeot-Talbot) ⑤ **Gar. de l'Eglise** (Ford) ⑥ **Couesnon** (Renault)
Banques	⑦ **Crédit Lyonnais** ⑧ **Société Générale** ⑨ **Crédit Agricole** ⑩ **Crédit Agricole**
	⑪ **Caisse d'Epargne** ⑫ **BNP** ⑬ **Société Générale**
S/marché	⑭ **Intermarché** ⑮ **Maxicoop** ⑯ **Lion**
Camping	⑰ **Municipal les Tilleuls** 14160 Dives-s-Mer ☎ 31 91 25 21 F:9(mi)-3
	⑱ **Le Vert Pré** 14390 Cabourg ☎ 31 91 41 68 F:10-3
	⑲ **Le Clos Tranquille** 14810 Merville-Franceville-Plage ☎ 31 24 21 36 F:10-3

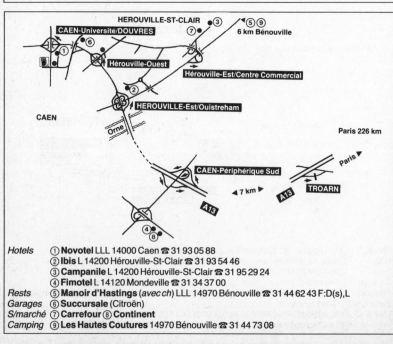

Hotels	① **Novotel** LLL 14000 Caen ☎ 31 93 05 88
	② **Ibis** L 14200 Hérouville-St-Clair ☎ 31 93 54 46
	③ **Campanile** L 14200 Hérouville-St-Clair ☎ 31 95 29 24
	④ **Fimotel** L 14120 Mondeville ☎ 31 34 37 00
Rests	⑤ **Manoir d'Hastings** (*avec ch*) LLL 14970 Bénouville ☎ 31 44 62 43 F:D(s),L
Garages	⑥ **Succursale** (Citroën)
S/marché	⑦ **Carrefour** ⑧ **Continent**
Camping	⑨ **Les Hautes Coutures** 14970 Bénouville ☎ 31 44 73 08

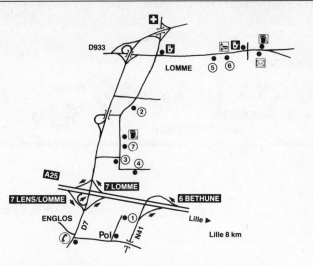

Hotels   ① **Novotel Lille Lomme** LLL Englos, 59320 Haubourdin ☎ 20 07 09 99
② **Mercure Lille Lomme** LLL Englos, 59320 Haubourdin ☎ 20 92 30 15
Garages   ③ **Eurauto** (Opel) ④ **de l'Heurtebise** (Renault)
Banques   ⑤ **Crédit Nord** ⑥ **Crédit Agricole**
S/marché   ⑦ **Auchan**

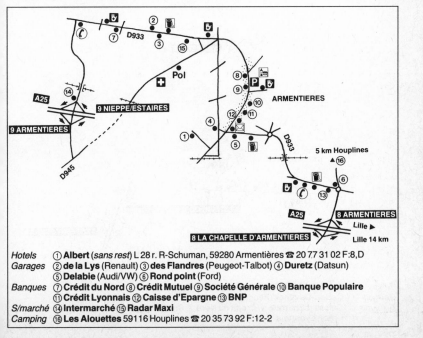

Hotels   ① **Albert** (*sans rest*) L 28 r. R-Schuman, 59280 Armentières ☎ 20 77 31 02 F:8,D
Garages   ② **de la Lys** (Renault) ③ **des Flandres** (Peugeot-Talbot) ④ **Duretz** (Datsun)
⑤ **Delabie** (Audi/VW) ⑥ **Rond point** (Ford)
Banques   ⑦ **Crédit du Nord** ⑧ **Crédit Mutuel** ⑨ **Société Générale** ⑩ **Banque Populaire**
⑪ **Crédit Lyonnais** ⑫ **Caisse d'Epargne** ⑬ **BNP**
S/marché   ⑭ **Intermarché** ⑮ **Radar Maxi**
Camping   ⑯ **Les Alouettes** 59116 Houplines ☎ 20 35 73 92 F:12-2

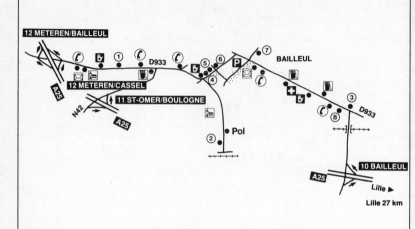

Garages ① **Plancke** (Audi/VW) ② **Duquesne** (Fiat) ③ **Tronet** (Citroën)
Banques ④ **Société Générale** ⑤ **BNP** ⑥ **Crédit Mutuel** ⑦ **Crédit Agricole**
S/marché ⑧ **Intermarché**

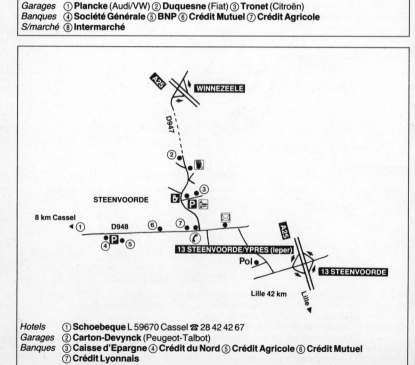

Hotels ① **Schoebeque** L 59670 Cassel ☎ 28 42 42 67
Garages ② **Carton-Devynck** (Peugeot-Talbot)
Banques ③ **Caisse d'Epargne** ④ **Crédit du Nord** ⑤ **Crédit Agricole** ⑥ **Crédit Mutuel**
⑦ **Crédit Lyonnais**

Hotels ① **Mercure** LL Lac d'Armbouts-Cappel, 59380 Bergues ☎ 28 60 70 60
② **Tonnelier** L 59380 Bergues ☎ 28 68 70 05 F:1,8(mi)-9(mi),V
③ **Commerce** (*sans rest*) L 59380 Bergues ☎ 28 68 60 37 F:7, 12-1(mi)
Garages ④ **Faubourg** (Peugeot-Talbot)
Banques ⑤ **Crédit Agricole** ⑥ **Société Générale** ⑦ **Caisse d'Epargne** ⑧ **Crédit Lyonnais**
S/marché ⑨ **Intermarché**
Camping ⑩ **La Becque** Warhem, 59380 Bergues ☎ 28 68 20 19 F:11-3

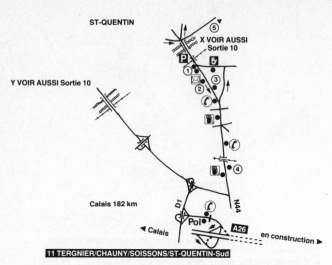

11 TERGNIER/CHAUNY/SOISSONS/ST-QUENTIN-Sud

Banques ① **Crédit du Nord** ② **Caisse d'Epargne** ③ **BNP**
S/marché ④ **Leclerc**
Camping ⑤ **Municipal** 02100 St-Quentin ☎ 23 62 68 66 F:12-2

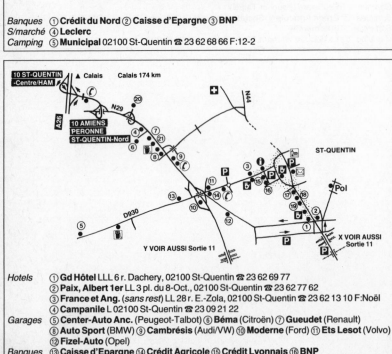

Hotels ① **Gd Hôtel** LLL 6 r. Dachery, 02100 St-Quentin ☎ 23 62 69 77
② **Paix, Albert 1er** LL 3 pl. du 8-Oct., 02100 St-Quentin ☎ 23 62 77 62
③ **France et Ang.** (*sans rest*) LL 28 r. E.-Zola, 02100 St-Quentin ☎ 23 62 13 10 F:Noël
④ **Campanile** L 02100 St-Quentin ☎ 23 09 21 22
Garages ⑤ **Center-Auto Anc.** (Peugeot-Talbot) ⑥ **Béma** (Citroën) ⑦ **Gueudet** (Renault)
⑧ **Auto Sport** (BMW) ⑨ **Cambrésis** (Audi/VW) ⑩ **Moderne** (Ford) ⑪ **Ets Lesot** (Volvo)
⑫ **Fizel-Auto** (Opel)
Banques ⑬ **Caisse d'Epargne** ⑭ **Crédit Agricole** ⑮ **Crédit Lyonnais** ⑯ **BNP**
⑰ **Crédit du Nord** ⑱ **Crédit Mutuel** ⑲ **Société Générale**
S/marché ⑳ **Mammouth** ㉑ **Intermarché**

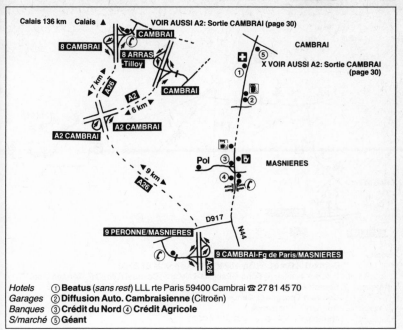

Hotels   ① **Beatus** (*sans rest*) LLL rte Paris 59400 Cambrai ☎ 27 81 45 70
Garages   ② **Diffusion Auto. Cambraisienne** (Citroën)
Banques   ③ **Crédit du Nord** ④ **Crédit Agricole**
S/marché ⑤ **Géant**

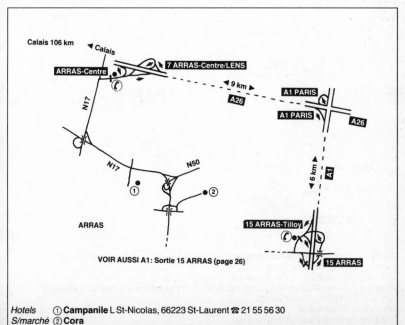

Hotels   ① **Campanile** L St-Nicolas, 66223 St-Laurent ☎ 21 55 56 30
S/marché ② **Cora**

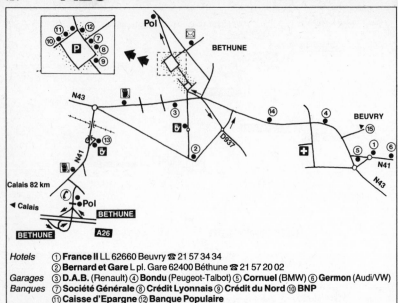

Hotels ① **France II** LL 62660 Beuvry ☎ 21 57 34 34
      ② **Bernard et Gare** L pl. Gare 62400 Béthune ☎ 21 57 20 02
Garages ③ **D.A.B.** (Renault) ④ **Bondu** (Peugeot-Talbot) ⑤ **Cornuel** (BMW) ⑥ **Germon** (Audi/VW)
Banques ⑦ **Société Générale** ⑧ **Crédit Lyonnais** ⑨ **Crédit du Nord** ⑩ **BNP**
      ⑪ **Caisse d'Epargne** ⑫ **Banque Populaire**
S/marché ⑬ **Auchan** ⑭ **Champion**
Camping ⑮ **Municipal** 62660 Beuvry ☎ 21 57 02 01

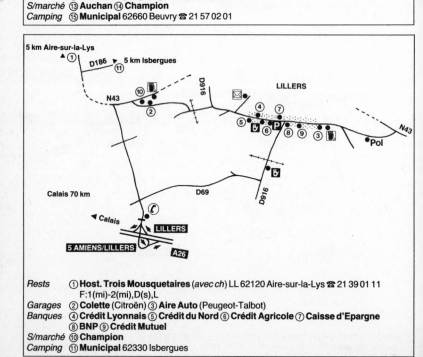

Rests ① **Host. Trois Mousquetaires** (*avec ch*) LL 62120 Aire-sur-la-Lys ☎ 21 39 01 11
      F:1(mi)-2(mi),D(s),L
Garages ② **Colette** (Citroën) ③ **Aire Auto** (Peugeot-Talbot)
Banques ④ **Crédit Lyonnais** ⑤ **Crédit du Nord** ⑥ **Crédit Agricole** ⑦ **Caisse d'Epargne**
      ⑧ **BNP** ⑨ **Crédit Mutuel**
S/marché ⑩ **Champion**
Camping ⑪ **Municipal** 62330 Isbergues

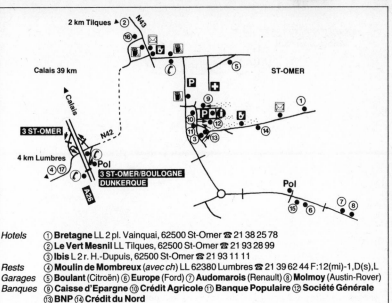

Hotels
① **Bretagne** LL 2 pl. Vainquai, 62500 St-Omer ☎ 21 38 25 78
② **Le Vert Mesnil** LL Tilques, 62500 St-Omer ☎ 21 93 28 99
③ **Ibis** L 2 r. H.-Dupuis, 62500 St-Omer ☎ 21 93 11 11
Rests ④ **Moulin de Mombreux** (*avec ch*) LL 62380 Lumbres ☎ 21 39 62 44 F:12(mi)-1,D(s),L
Garages ⑤ **Boulant** (Citroën) ⑥ **Europe** (Ford) ⑦ **Audomarois** (Renault) ⑧ **Molmoy** (Austin-Rover)
Banques ⑨ **Caisse d'Epargne** ⑩ **Crédit Agricole** ⑪ **Banque Populaire** ⑫ **Société Générale**
⑬ **BNP** ⑭ **Crédit du Nord**
S/marché ⑮ **Mammouth** ⑯ **PG**
Camping ⑰ **Municipal** 62380 Lumbres F:10-4

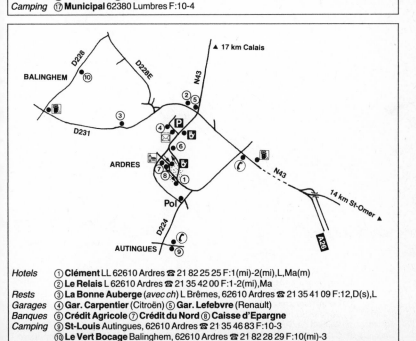

Hotels
① **Clément** LL 62610 Ardres ☎ 21 82 25 25 F:1(mi)-2(mi),L,Ma(m)
② **Le Relais** L 62610 Ardres ☎ 21 35 42 00 F:1-2(mi),Ma
Rests ③ **La Bonne Auberge** (*avec ch*) L Brêmes, 62610 Ardres ☎ 21 35 41 09 F:12,D(s),L
Garages ④ **Gar. Carpentier** (Citroën) ⑤ **Gar. Lefebvre** (Renault)
Banques ⑥ **Crédit Agricole** ⑦ **Crédit du Nord** ⑧ **Caisse d'Epargne**
Camping ⑨ **St-Louis** Autingues, 62610 Ardres ☎ 21 35 46 83 F:10-3
⑩ **Le Vert Bocage** Balinghem, 62610 Ardres ☎ 21 82 28 29 F:10(mi)-3

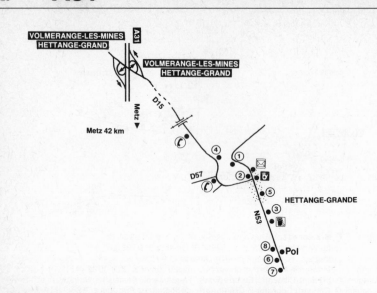

Garages ① **Aubry** (Citroën) ② **Diettert** (Audi/VW) ③ **Sandt** (Renault)
Banques ④ **Caisse d'Epargne** ⑤ **Crédit Mutuel** ⑥ **Banque Populaire** ⑦ **Crédit Agricole**
S/marché ⑧ **SGAF**

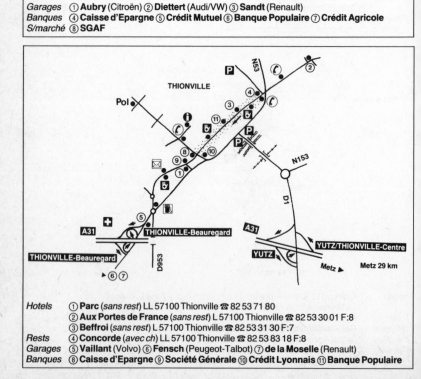

Hotels ① **Parc** (*sans rest*) LL 57100 Thionville ☎ 82 53 71 80
    ② **Aux Portes de France** (*sans rest*) L 57100 Thionville ☎ 82 53 30 01 F:8
    ③ **Beffroi** (*sans rest*) L 57100 Thionville ☎ 82 53 31 30 F:7
Rests ④ **Concorde** (*avec ch*) LL 57100 Thionville ☎ 82 53 83 18 F:8
Garages ⑤ **Vaillant** (Volvo) ⑥ **Fensch** (Peugeot-Talbot) ⑦ **de la Moselle** (Renault)
Banques ⑧ **Caisse d'Epargne** ⑨ **Société Générale** ⑩ **Crédit Lyonnais** ⑪ **Banque Populaire**

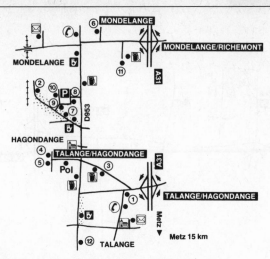

Hotels	① **Climat de France** L Talange, 57300 Hagondange ☎ 87 72 13 11	
Rests	② **Méligner** L 57300 Hagondange ☎ 87 71 47 53 F:8,S	
Garages	③ **Parachini** (Fiat) ④ **Blanquier** (Toyota) ⑤ **Gentile** (Citroën)	
	⑥ **Mondelange Auto** (Peugeot-Talbot)	
Banques	⑦ **BNP** ⑧ **Caisse d'Epargne** ⑨ **Crédit Agricole** ⑩ **Crédit Lyonnais**	
S/marché	⑪ **Cora** ⑫ **Super U**	

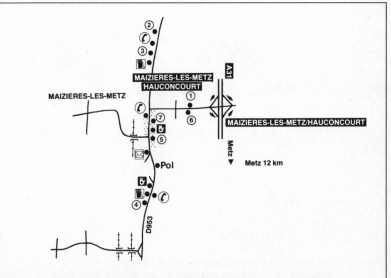

Hotels	① **Novotel** LLL 57210 Maizières-lès-Metz ☎ 87 80 41 11	
Garages	② **Bommersheim** (Renault) ③ **Bohnenberger** (Peugeot-Talbot) ④ **Magra** (Citroën)	
Banques	⑤ **Crédit Lyonnais**	
S/marché	⑥ **Leclerc** ⑦ **Super U**	

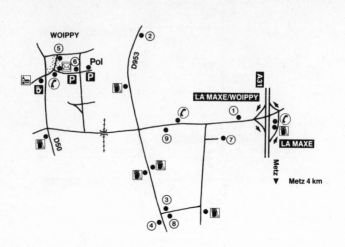

Hotels ① **Mercure** LLL 57140 Woippy ☎ 87 32 52 79
Garages ② **Renault-Woippy** (Renault) ③ **Jacquot** (Peugeot-Talbot) ④ **Succursale** (Mercedes)
Banques ⑤ **Crédit Agricole** ⑥ **Crédit Mutuel**
S/marché ⑦ **Rond point** ⑧ **Intermarché** ⑨ **Super U**

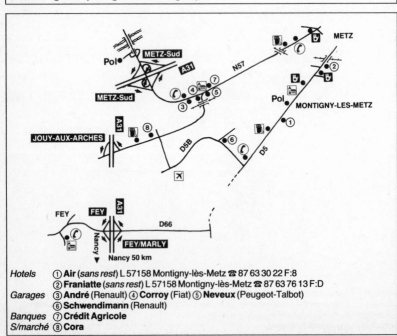

Hotels ① **Air** (*sans rest*) L 57158 Montigny-lès-Metz ☎ 87 63 30 22 F:8
 ② **Franiatte** (*sans rest*) L 57158 Montigny-lès-Metz ☎ 87 63 76 13 F:D
Garages ③ **André** (Renault) ④ **Corroy** (Fiat) ⑤ **Neveux** (Peugeot-Talbot)
 ⑥ **Schwendimann** (Renault)
Banques ⑦ **Crédit Agricole**
S/marché ⑧ **Cora**

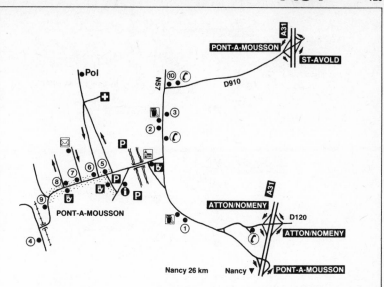

Garages ① **Fasse** (Citroën) ② **Toulouse Autos** (Ford) ③ **Martin** (Audi/VW) ④ **André** (Peug-Talb)
Banques ⑤ **BNP** ⑥ **Banque Populaire** ⑦ **Crédit Lyonnais** ⑧ **Soc. Gén** ⑨ **Caisse d'Epargne**
S/marché ⑩ **Record**

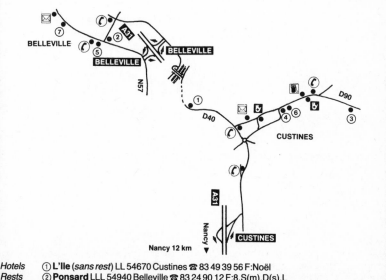

Hotels ① **L'Ile** (*sans rest*) LL 54670 Custines ☎ 83 49 39 56 F:Noël
Rests ② **Ponsard** LLL 54940 Belleville ☎ 83 24 90 12 F:8,S(m),D(s),L
Garages ③ **Kauffmann** (Renault)
Banques ④ **Crédit Agricole** ⑤ **Caisse d'Epargne**
S/marché ⑥ **Champion** ⑦ **Unico**

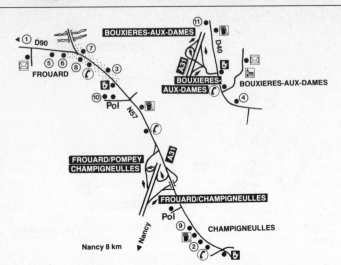

Rests ① **des Vannes et sa Résidence** (*avec ch*) LLL 54460 Liverdun ☎ 83 24 46 01
　　　　F:2-3(mi),L,Ma(m)
Garages ② **Ruer** (Ford) ③ **Maillefort** (Peugeot-Talbot) ④ **Guerin** (Renault)
Banques ⑤ **Caisse d'Epargne** ⑥ **Crédit Agricole** ⑦ **Banque Populaire** ⑧ **Société Générale**
S/marché ⑨ **GRO** ⑩ **Migros** ⑪ **SGAF**

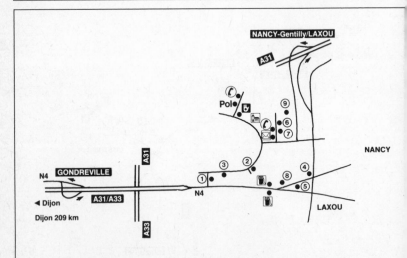

Hotels ① **Novotel Nancy Ouest** LLL 54520 Laxou ☎ 83 96 67 46
　　　　② **Ariane** LL 54520 Laxou ☎ 83 98 37 10
Garages ③ **GDA** (Audi/VW) ④ **Succursale** (Renault) ⑤ **S.I.A.L.** (Peugeot-Talbot)
Banques ⑥ **Caisse d'Epargne** ⑦ **Banque Populaire** ⑧ **Crédit Agricole**
S/marché ⑨ **Rond point**

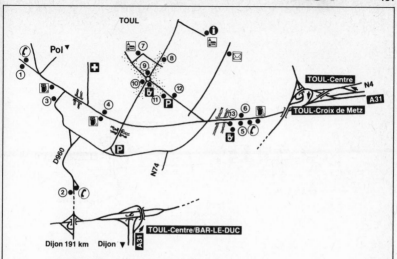

Hotels   ① **Europe** (*sans rest*) L 54200 Toul ☎ 83 43 00 10 F:2
Garages   ② **Mathiot-Meny** (Peugeot-Talbot) ③ **St-Eyre** (Fiat) ④ **Remparts** (Ford)
          ⑤ **Sinard** (Renault) ⑥ **St-Martin** (Audi/VW)
Banques   ⑦ **Banque Populaire** ⑧ **BNP** ⑨ **Crédit Lyonnais** ⑩ **Crédit Agricole** ⑪ **Crédit Mutuel**
          ⑫ **Caisse d'Epargne**
S/marché   ⑬ **Leclerc**

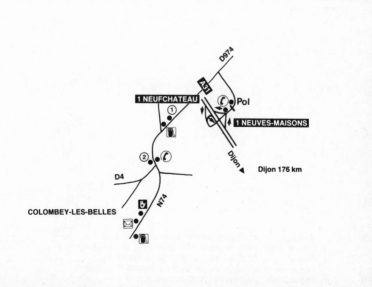

Garages   ① **Esso** (Renault)
Banques   ② **Crédit Agricole**

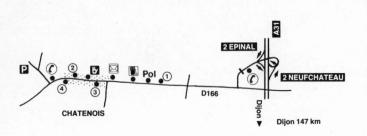

Garages ① **Gilbert** (Renault) ② **Adam** (Peugeot-Talbot)
Banques ③ **Caisse d'Epargne** ④ **Banque Klob**

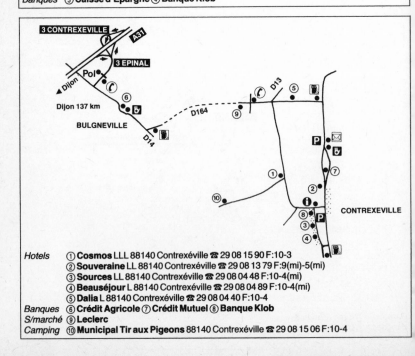

Hotels	① **Cosmos** LLL 88140 Contrexéville ☎ 29 08 15 90 F:10-3
	② **Souveraine** LL 88140 Contrexéville ☎ 29 08 13 79 F:9(mi)-5(mi)
	③ **Sources** LL 88140 Contrexéville ☎ 29 08 04 48 F:10-4(mi)
	④ **Beauséjour** L 88140 Contrexéville ☎ 29 08 04 89 F:10-4(mi)
	⑤ **Dalia** L 88140 Contrexéville ☎ 29 08 04 40 F:10-4
Banques	⑥ **Crédit Agricole** ⑦ **Crédit Mutuel** ⑧ **Banque Klob**
S/marché	⑨ **Leclerc**
Camping	⑩ **Municipal Tir aux Pigeons** 88140 Contrexéville ☎ 29 08 15 06 F:10-4

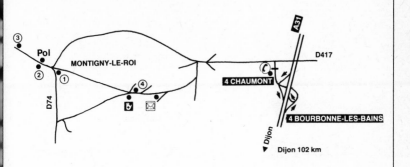

Hotels   ① **Moderne** L Montigny-le-Roi, 52140 Le Val de Meuse ☎ 25 86 10 18
Garages   ② **Rabert et fils** (Renault) ③ **Flagez** (Peugeot-Talbot)
Banques   ④ **Crédit Agricole**

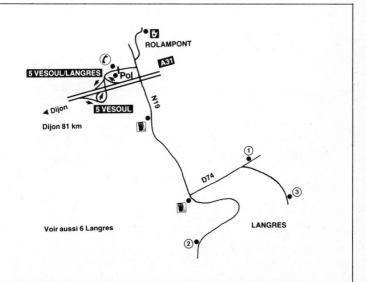

Hotels   ① **La Grange au Prieur** LL 52200 Langres ☎ 25 85 10 27 F:11(mi)-12(mi),D(s),L(m)
Garages   ② **Europe** (Audi/VW)
S/marché   ③ **Rond point**

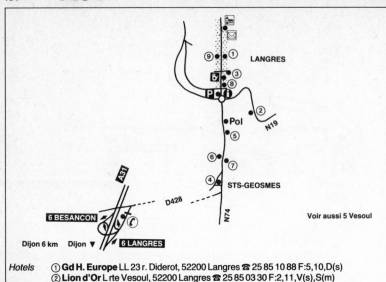

Hotels   ① **Gd H. Europe** LL 23 r. Diderot, 52200 Langres ☎ 25 85 10 88 F:5,10,D(s)
           ② **Lion d'Or** L rte Vesoul, 52200 Langres ☎ 25 85 03 30 F:2,11,V(s),S(m)
           ③ **Cheval Blanc** L 4 r. Estrés, 52200 Langres ☎ 25 85 07 00 F:1,Me
Rests   ④ **Aub. des 3 Jumeaux** (*avec ch*) LL Sts-Geosmes, 52200 Langres ☎ 25 85 03 36 F:11,L
Garages ⑤ **Noirot** (Ford) ⑥ **Perin** (Citroën) ⑦ **Berthier** (Peugeot-Talbot)
Banques ⑧ **Crédit Mutuel** ⑨ **Société Générale**

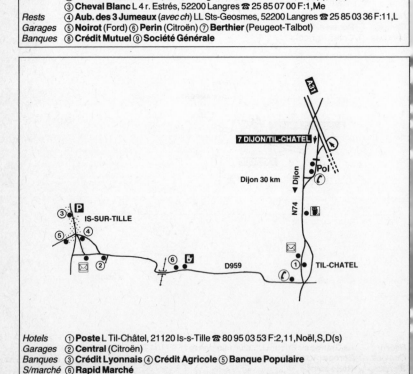

Hotels   ① **Poste** L Til-Châtel, 21120 Is-s-Tille ☎ 80 95 03 53 F:2,11,Noël,S,D(s)
Garages   ② **Central** (Citroën)
Banques   ③ **Crédit Lyonnais** ④ **Crédit Agricole** ⑤ **Banque Populaire**
S/marché ⑥ **Rapid Marché**

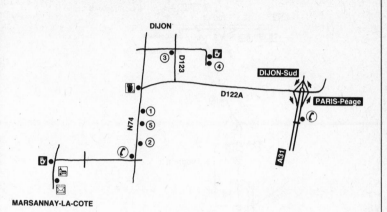

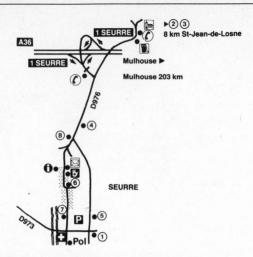

Hotels
① **Le Castel** LL 21250 Seurre ☎ 80 20 45 07 F:1,L(10-6)
② **Aub. de la Marine** L Losne, 21170 St-Jean-de-Losne ☎ 80 29 05 11 F:12-1
③ **Saônotel** L 21170 St-Jean-de-Losne ☎ 80 29 04 77 F:11,V(10-3)

Garages ④ **Seurre Auto** (Ford) ⑤ **Garage Berbey** (Renault)

Banques ⑥ **Crédit Agricole** ⑦ **BNP**

S/marché ⑧ **Maximarché**

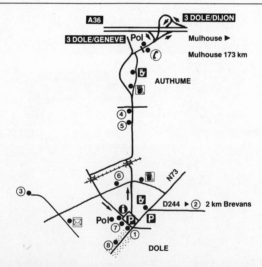

Hotels
① **Grand Hôtel Chandioux** LLL pl. Grévy, 39100 Dole ☎ 84 79 00 66
② **Au Village** L Brévans, 39100 Dole ☎ 84 72 56 40 F:Noël

Rests ③ **Buffet Gare** L 39100 Dole ☎ 84 82 00 48 F:J(s)

Garages ④ **Tavernier** (Alfa-Datsun) ⑤ **Dole-Auto** (Peugeot-Talbot) ⑥ **Morilhat** (Renault)

Banques ⑦ **Banque Populaire** ⑧ **Crédit Agricole**

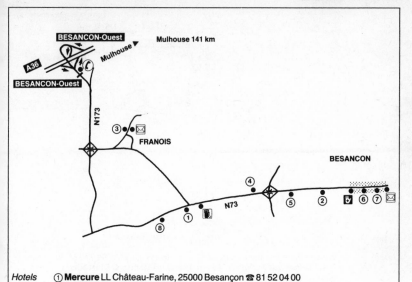

Hotels   ① **Mercure** LL Château-Farine, 25000 Besançon ☎ 81 52 04 00
Rests   ② **Le Chaudanne** LL (*dej. seul.*) 25000 Besançon ☎ 81 52 06 13 F:2,Noël,D
Garages   ③ **Trouttet** (Renault) ④ **Succursale** (Citroën) ⑤ **Girard** (Peugeot-Talbot)
Banques   ⑥ **Banque Populaire** ⑦ **Crédit Mutuel**
S/marché   ⑧ **Mammouth**

Hotels   ① **Novotel** LLL r. Trey, 25000 Besançon ☎ 81 50 14 66
    ② **Campanile** L Ecole-Valentin, 25480 Miserey Salines ☎ 81 53 52 22
Rests   ③ **Valentin** LL 25480 Miserey Salines ☎ 81 55 31 62 F:2,8,D(s),L
Garages   ④ **Dunand** (Renault) ⑤ **Maisonnettes** (Citroën)
Banques   ⑥ **Crédit Agricole** ⑦ **Banque Populaire** ⑧ **Société Générale**
S/marché   ⑨ **Carrefour**
Camping   ⑩ **Geneuille** 25870 Geneuille ☎ 81 57 72 04 F:10(mi)-4(mi)

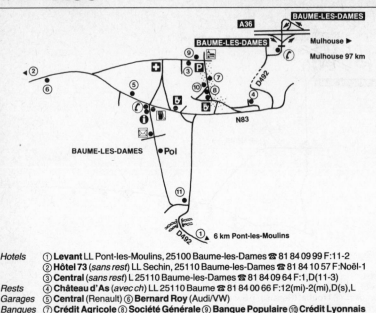

Hotels
① **Levant** LL Pont-les-Moulins, 25100 Baume-les-Dames ☎ 81 84 09 99 F:11-2
② **Hôtel 73** (*sans rest*) LL Sechin, 25110 Baume-les-Dames ☎ 81 84 10 57 F:Noël-1
③ **Central** (*sans rest*) L 25110 Baume-les-Dames ☎ 81 84 09 64 F:1,D(11-3)
Rests ④ **Château d'As** (*avec ch*) LL 25110 Baume ☎ 81 84 00 66 F:12(mi)-2(mi),D(s),L
Garages ⑤ **Central** (Renault) ⑥ **Bernard Roy** (Audi/VW)
Banques ⑦ **Crédit Agricole** ⑧ **Société Générale** ⑨ **Banque Populaire** ⑩ **Crédit Lyonnais**
S/marché ⑪ **Suma**

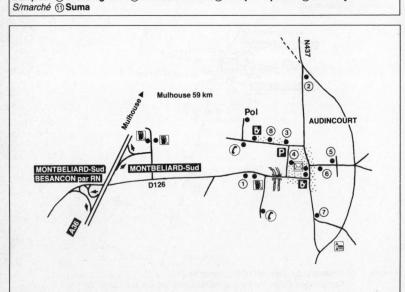

Garages ① **Sacma** (Opel) ② **Succursale** (Peugeot-Talbot)
Banques ③ **BNP** ④ **Société Générale** ⑤ **Banque Populaire** ⑥ **Caisse d'Epargne**
⑦ **Crédit Agricole**
S/marché ⑧ **Prisunic**

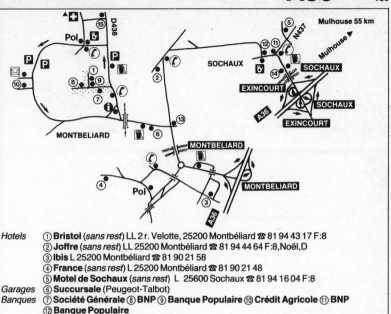

Hotels	
Hotels	① **Bristol** (*sans rest*) LL 2 r. Velotte, 25200 Montbéliard ☎ 81 94 43 17 F:8
	② **Joffre** (*sans rest*) LL 25200 Montbéliard ☎ 81 94 44 64 F:8,Noël,D
	③ **Ibis** L 25200 Montbéliard ☎ 81 90 21 58
	④ **France** (*sans rest*) L 25200 Montbéliard ☎ 81 90 21 48
	⑤ **Motel de Sochaux** (*sans rest*) L 25600 Sochaux ☎ 81 94 16 04 F:8
Garages	⑥ **Succursale** (Peugeot-Talbot)
Banques	⑦ **Société Générale** ⑧ **BNP** ⑨ **Banque Populaire** ⑩ **Crédit Agricole** ⑪ **BNP**
	⑫ **Banque Populaire**
S/marché	⑬ **Super Ravi** ⑭ **Super Ravi** ⑮ **Suma**

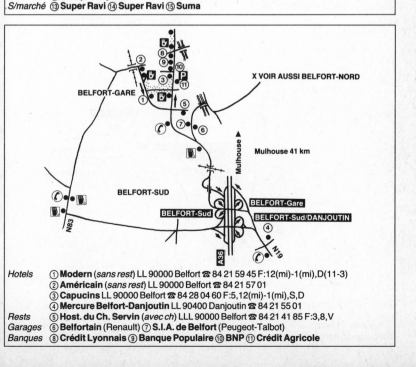

X VOIR AUSSI BELFORT-NORD

Hotels	
Hotels	① **Modern** (*sans rest*) LL 90000 Belfort ☎ 84 21 59 45 F:12(mi)-1(mi),D(11-3)
	② **Américain** (*sans rest*) LL 90000 Belfort ☎ 84 21 57 01
	③ **Capucins** LL 90000 Belfort ☎ 84 28 04 60 F:5,12(mi)-1(mi),S,D
	④ **Mercure Belfort-Danjoutin** LL 90400 Danjoutin ☎ 84 21 55 01
Rests	⑤ **Host. du Ch. Servin** (*avec ch*) LLL 90000 Belfort ☎ 84 21 41 85 F:3,8,V
Garages	⑥ **Belfortain** (Renault) ⑦ **S.I.A. de Belfort** (Peugeot-Talbot)
Banques	⑧ **Crédit Lyonnais** ⑨ **Banque Populaire** ⑩ **BNP** ⑪ **Crédit Agricole**

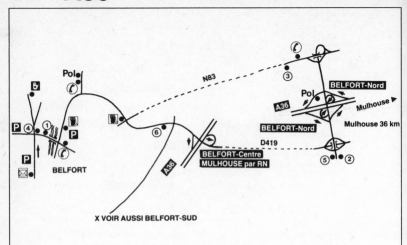

X VOIR AUSSI BELFORT-SUD

Hotels ① **Grand Hôtel du Lion** LLL 90000 Belfort ☎ 84 21 17 00
② **Campanile** L 90160 Bessoncourt ☎ 84 22 12 56
Garages ③ **Melin** (Mercedes)
Banques ④ **Caisse d'Epargne**
S/marché ⑤ **Euromarché** ⑥ **Suma**

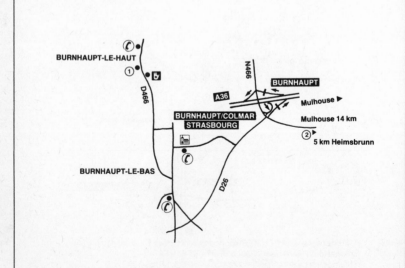

S/marché ① **Unico**
Camping ② **Parc la Chaumière** 68990 Heimsbrunn ☎ 89 81 93 43

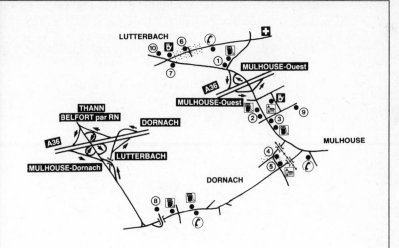

Hotels   ① **Campanile** L 68460 Lutterbach ☎ 89 53 66 55
Garages   ② **Muller** (Opel) ③ **S.I.A.M.** (Peugeot-Talbot)
Banques   ④ **Banque Populaire** ⑤ **Crédit Mutuel** ⑥ **Société Générale** ⑦ **Banque Populaire**
S/marché ⑧ **Hyper** ⑨ **Ravi** ⑩ **Coop**

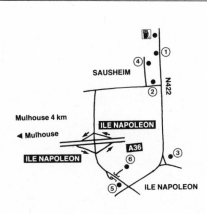

Hotels   ① **Sofitel** LLL 68390 Sausheim ☎ 89 44 75 75
         ② **Novotel Mulhouse-Sausheim** LLL ☎ 89 44 44 44
         ③ **Mercure Mulhouse-Sausheim** LLL ☎ 89 44 54 40
         ④ **Ibis Mulhouse-Sausheim** L ☎ 89 54 32 33
Garages   ⑤ **S.I.A.M.** (Peugeot-Talbot)
S/marché ⑥ **Euromarché**

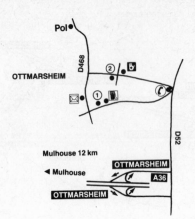

Garages ① **Liebenguth** (Renault)
Banques ② **Crédit Agricole**

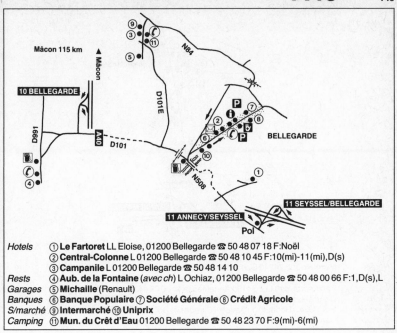

Hotels	① **Le Fartoret** LL Eloise, 01200 Bellegarde ☎ 50 48 07 18 F:Noël	
	② **Central-Colonne** L 01200 Bellegarde ☎ 50 48 10 45 F:10(mi)-11(mi),D(s)	
	③ **Campanile** L 01200 Bellegarde ☎ 50 48 14 10	
Rests	④ **Aub. de la Fontaine** (*avec ch*) L Ochiaz, 01200 Bellegarde ☎ 50 48 00 66 F:1,D(s),L	
Garages	⑤ **Michaille** (Renault)	
Banques	⑥ **Banque Populaire** ⑦ **Société Générale** ⑧ **Crédit Agricole**	
S/marché	⑨ **Intermarché** ⑩ **Uniprix**	
Camping	⑪ **Mun. du Crêt d'Eau** 01200 Bellegarde ☎ 50 48 23 70 F:9(mi)-6(mi)	

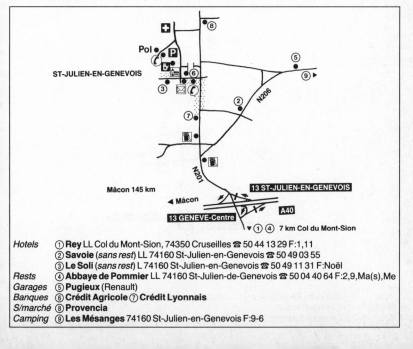

ST-JULIEN-EN-GENEVOIS

Mâcon 145 km

◄ Mâcon

13 ST-JULIEN-EN-GENEVOIS

13 GENEVE-Centre

A40

▼ ① ④ 7 km Col du Mont-Sion

Hotels	① **Rey** LL Col du Mont-Sion, 74350 Cruseilles ☎ 50 44 13 29 F:1,11	
	② **Savoie** (*sans rest*) LL 74160 St-Julien-en-Genevois ☎ 50 49 03 55	
	③ **Le Soli** (*sans rest*) L 74160 St-Julien-en-Genevois ☎ 50 49 11 31 F:Noël	
Rests	④ **Abbaye de Pommier** LL 74160 St-Julien-de-Genevois ☎ 50 04 40 64 F:2,9,Ma(s),Me	
Garages	⑤ **Pugieux** (Renault)	
Banques	⑥ **Crédit Agricole** ⑦ **Crédit Lyonnais**	
S/marché	⑧ **Provencia**	
Camping	⑨ **Les Mésanges** 74160 St-Julien-en-Genevois F:9-6	

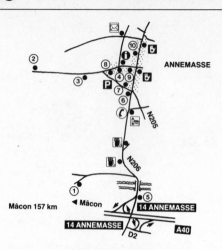

ANNEMASSE

N205

N206

Mâcon 157 km

◄ Mâcon

14 ANNEMASSE

14 ANNEMASSE

A40

D2

Hotels ① **Mercure** LLL 74240 Gaillard ☎ 50 92 05 25
② **Helvetia** LLL 74100 Annemasse ☎ 50 38 59 80
③ **Parc** (*sans rest*) LLL 74100 Annemasse ☎ 50 38 44 60
④ **Central** (*sans rest*) LL 74100 Annemasse ☎ 50 38 27 06
Garages ⑤ **S.A.D.I.A.** (Renault) ⑥ **Savoie** (Citroën) ⑦ **Bel** (Opel)
Banques ⑧ **Caisse d'Epargne** ⑨ **Société Générale** ⑩ **Banque Savoie**

D903 ③ ☒ D907

① ④ **BONNE**

FINDROL

N205 ②

Mâcon 166 km ◄ Mâcon

THONON/EVIAN

LA ROCHE-S-FORON

N503 **A40**

Rests ① **Jardin de Paris** (*avec ch*) LL 74380 Bonne ☎ 50 39 20 15 F:6,Ma
Garages ② **Busato** (Renault)
Banques ③ **Caisse d'Epargne** ④ **Crédit Agricole**

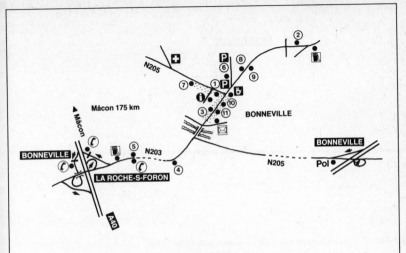

Hotels ① **Sapeur** LLL 74130 Bonneville ☎ 50 97 20 68 F:6,8,Noël,D(s),L
      ② **Alpes** LL 74130 Bonneville ☎ 50 97 10 47 F:7,12
      ③ **Arve** LL 74130 Bonneville ☎ 50 97 01 28 F:9,S
Garages ④ **Andréoléty** (Peugeot-Talbot) ⑤ **SECAPA** (Audi/VW)
Banques ⑥ **Caisse d'Epargne** ⑦ **Crédit Lyonnais** ⑧ **Banque Populaire** ⑨ **Crédit Agricole**
      ⑩ **BNP** ⑪ **Société Générale**

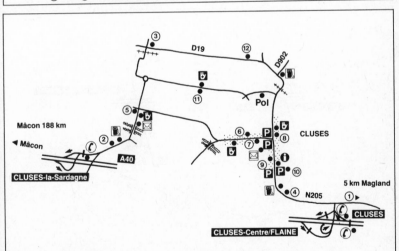

Rests ① **Relais Mont-Blanc** (*avec ch*) L Magland, 74300 Cluses ☎ 50 90 75 33 F:1
Garages ② **Fillon** (Audi/VW) ③ **Savoie** (Peugeot-Talbot) ④ **Gander** (Ford)
Banques ⑤ **Crédit Lyonnais** ⑥ **Crédit Lyonnais** ⑦ **BNP** ⑧ **Banque Populaire**
      ⑨ **Société Générale** ⑩ **Crédit Agricole**
S/marché ⑪ **Provencia**
Camping ⑫ **La Corbaz** 74300 Cluses ☎ 50 98 44 03

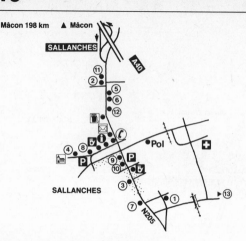

Hotels
① **Les Sorbiers** LL 74700 Sallanches ☎ 50 58 01 22
② **Ibis** L 74700 Sallanches ☎ 50 58 14 42
③ **Mont-Blanc** (*sans rest*) L 74700 Sallanches ☎ 50 58 12 47
④ **St-Jacques** (*sans rest*) L 74700 Sallanches ☎ 50 58 01 35
Garages ⑤ **Greffoz** (Citroën) ⑥ **Warens** (Peugeot-Talbot) ⑦ **Alpes** (Ford)
Banques ⑧ **Crédit Lyonnais** ⑨ **Caisse d'Epargne** ⑩ **BNP**
S/marché ⑪ **Record** ⑫ **Codec**
Camping ⑬ **Mt-Blanc-Village** 74700 Sallanches ☎ 50 58 43 67 F:9(mi)-3

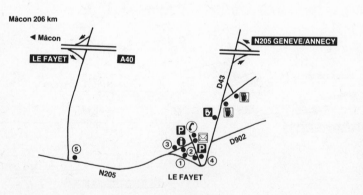

Hotels
① **La Chaumière** LL 74190 Le Fayet ☎ 50 78 15 88 F:10-Noël
② **Central** (*sans rest*) L 74190 Le Fayet ☎ 50 78 15 99 F:5,10(mi)-11(mi)
Banques ③ **Banque Laydernier** ④ **Crédit Agricole**
S/marché ⑤ **Le Forum**

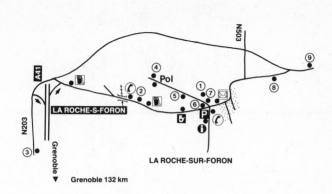

Hotels ① **Les Afforets** LL 74800 La Roche-sur-Foron ☎ 50 03 35 01 F:D
Garages ② **Bouvard** (Ford) ③ **Desbiolles** (Citroën) ④ **Duret** (Peugeot-Talbot)
Banques ⑤ **Caisse d'Epargne** ⑥ **Crédit Agricole** ⑦ **Banque Populaire**
S/marché ⑧ **Lion codec** ⑨ **Intermarché**

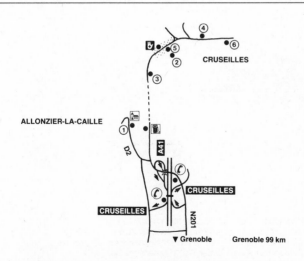

Hotels ① **Manoir** LL Allonzier, 74350 Cruseilles ☎ 50 46 81 82 F:11-Noël,L
    ② **Salève** LL 74350 Cruseilles ☎ 50 44 18 30 F:1,11,L
Garages ③ **Revillard** (Peugeot-Talbot) ④ **Bonhomme** (Citroën)
Banques ⑤ **Crédit Agricole**
Camping ⑥ **Parc des Dronières** 74350 Cruseilles ☎ 50 44 13 95 F:9-6

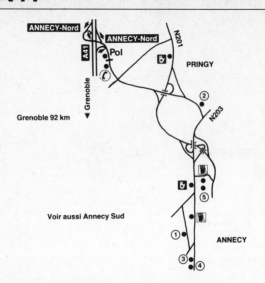

Hotels	① **Parc** (*sans rest*) L 43 ch. des Fins, 74000 Annecy ☎ 50 57 02 98 F:6,11,12
Rests	② **Fier** (*avec ch*) L Pont de Brogny, 74370 Pringy ☎ 50 46 11 10 F:11,Ma(s),Me
Banques	③ **Banque Laydernier** ④ **Crédit Agricole**
S/marché	⑤ **Carrefour**

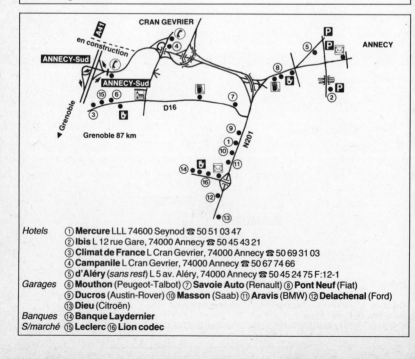

Hotels	① **Mercure** LLL 74600 Seynod ☎ 50 51 03 47
	② **Ibis** L 12 rue Gare, 74000 Annecy ☎ 50 45 43 21
	③ **Climat de France** L Cran Gevrier, 74000 Annecy ☎ 50 69 31 03
	④ **Campanile** L Cran Gevrier, 74000 Annecy ☎ 50 67 74 66
	⑤ **d'Aléry** (*sans rest*) L 5 av. Aléry, 74000 Annecy ☎ 50 45 24 75 F:12-1
Garages	⑥ **Mouthon** (Peugeot-Talbot) ⑦ **Savoie Auto** (Renault) ⑧ **Pont Neuf** (Fiat)
	⑨ **Ducros** (Austin-Rover) ⑩ **Masson** (Saab) ⑪ **Aravis** (BMW) ⑫ **Delachenal** (Ford)
	⑬ **Dieu** (Citroën)
Banques	⑭ **Banque Laydernier**
S/marché	⑮ **Leclerc** ⑯ **Lion codec**

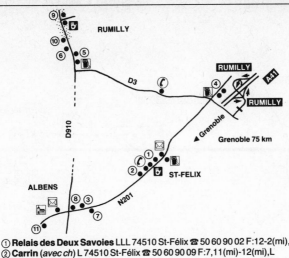

Hotels	① **Relais des Deux Savoies** LLL 74510 St-Félix ☎ 50 60 90 02 F:12-2(mi),Ma
Rests	② **Carrin** (*avec ch*) L 74510 St-Félix ☎ 50 60 90 09 F:7,11(mi)-12(mi),L
	③ **Aub. Fleurie** (*avec ch*) L 73410 Albens ☎ 79 63 00 18 F:3,11,L(s),Ma
Garages	④ **Provent** (Renault) ⑤ **Baudet** (Renault) ⑥ **Gantelet** (Peugeot-Talbot)
	⑦ **Gare** (Citroën) ⑧ **du Centre** (Peugeot-Talbot)
Banques	⑨ **Crédit Agricole**
S/marché	⑩ **Lion codec**
Camping	⑪ **Beauséjour** 73410 Albens F:9(mi)-6(mi)

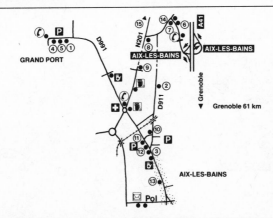

Hotels	① **La Pastorale** LLL Grand Port, 73100 Aix-les-Bains ☎ 79 35 25 36 F:2,3
	② **Soleil Couchant** L 73100 Aix-les-Bains ☎ 79 35 05 83 F:10(mi)-5(mi)
	③ **Palma** (*sans rest*) L 73100 Aix-les-Bains ☎ 79 35 01 10 F:11-4
Rests	④ **Lille** (*avec ch*) LLL Grand Port, 73100 Aix-les-Bains ☎ 79 35 04 22 F:1,2
	⑤ **Davat** (*avec ch*) LLL Grand Port, 73100 Aix-les-Bains ☎ 79 35 09 63 F:11-3,Ma
Garages	⑥ **S.A.S.** (Audi/VW) ⑦ **Celta** (Renault) ⑧ **Barrachin** (Peugeot-Talbot)
	⑨ **du Parc** (BMW) ⑩ **Perrel** (Renault)
Banques	⑪ **BNP** ⑫ **Crédit Agricole** ⑬ **Caisse d'Epargne**
S/marché	⑭ **Intermarché**
Camping	⑮ **Le Clos des Fourches** La Biolle, 73410 Albens ☎ 79 54 77 77

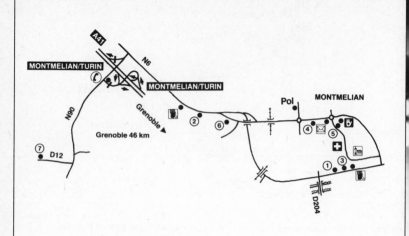

Hotels ① **George** L 73800 Montmélian ☎ 79 84 05 87 F:5,10-12(mi),Ma
Garages ② **Joquet** (Nissan) ③ **Novel** (Renault)
Banques ④ **Banque de Savoie** ⑤ **Crédit Agricole**
S/marché ⑥ **Super U**
Camping ⑦ **La Ferme du Lac** Les Marches, 73800 Montmélian ☎ 79 28 13 48 F:10-4(mi)

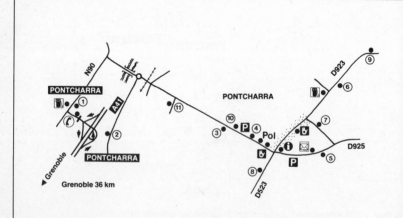

Hotels ① **Climat de France** L 38530 Pontcharra ☎ 76 71 91 84
Garages ② **Menetrey** (Audi/VW) ③ **Bayard** (Peugeot-Talbot) ④ **Camilleri** (Renault)
⑤ **Bricalli** (Peugeot-Talbot) ⑥ **St-Benoit** (Ford)
Banques ⑦ **Banque de Savoie** ⑧ **BNP**
S/marché ⑨ **Intermarché** ⑩ **Genty**
Camping ⑪ **Municipal** 38530 Pontcharra F:9(mi)-6(mi)

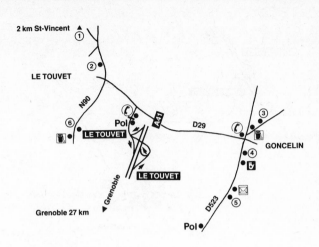

Hotels ① **Aub. St-Vincent** L St-Vincent, 38660 Le Touvet ☎ 76 08 46 97
Garages ② **Poulat** (Citroën) ③ **Couplaix** (Renault)
Banques ④ **Crédit Agricole** ⑤ **Caisse d'Epargne**
S/marché ⑥ **Intermarché**

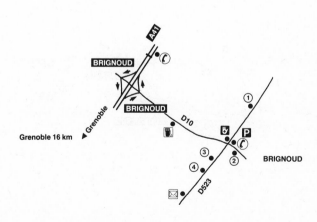

Garages ① **Brachi** (Renault)
Banques ② **Caisse d'Epargne** ③ **Société Générale** ④ **Crédit Agricole**

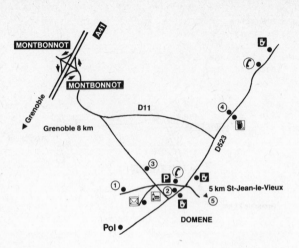

Hotels   ① **Le Beauvoir** L 38420 Domène ☎ 76 77 20 91
Banques   ② **BNP** ③ **Crédit Agricole**
S/marché   ④ **Genty**
Camping   ⑤ **Le Naysord** St-Jean-le-Vieux, 38420 Domène ☎ 76 77 12 37 F:11-4

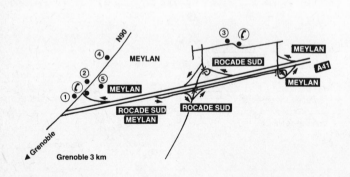

Hotels   ① **Alpha** LLL 38240 Meylan ☎ 76 90 63 09
           ② **Belle Vallée** (*sans rest*) LL 38240 Meylan ☎ 76 90 42 65
           ③ **Climat de France** L 38240 Meylan ☎ 76 90 76 90
Banques   ④ **Société Générale**
S/marché   ⑤ **Carrefour**

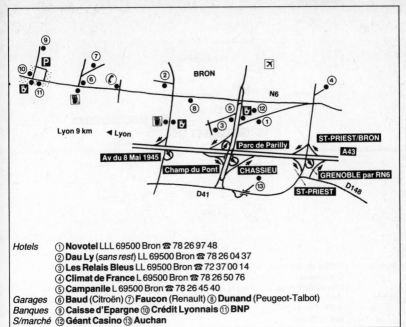

Hotels
- ① **Novotel** LLL 69500 Bron ☎ 78 26 97 48
- ② **Dau Ly** (*sans rest*) LL 69500 Bron ☎ 78 26 04 37
- ③ **Les Relais Bleus** LL 69500 Bron ☎ 72 37 00 14
- ④ **Climat de France** L 69500 Bron ☎ 78 26 50 76
- ⑤ **Campanile** L 69500 Bron ☎ 78 26 45 40

Garages
- ⑥ **Baud** (Citroën) ⑦ **Faucon** (Renault) ⑧ **Dunand** (Peugeot-Talbot)

Banques
- ⑨ **Caisse d'Epargne** ⑩ **Crédit Lyonnais** ⑪ **BNP**

S/marché
- ⑫ **Géant Casino** ⑬ **Auchan**

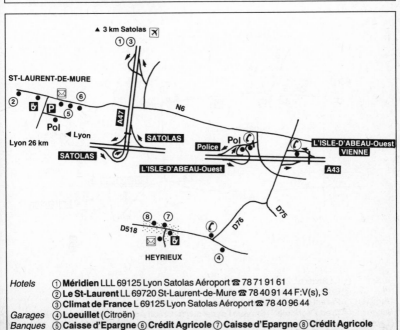

Hotels
- ① **Méridien** LLL 69125 Lyon Satolas Aéroport ☎ 78 71 91 61
- ② **Le St-Laurent** LL 69720 St-Laurent-de-Mure ☎ 78 40 91 44 F:V(s), S
- ③ **Climat de France** L 69125 Lyon Satolas Aéroport ☎ 78 40 96 44

Garages
- ④ **Loeuillet** (Citroën)

Banques
- ⑤ **Caisse d'Epargne** ⑥ **Crédit Agricole** ⑦ **Caisse d'Epargne** ⑧ **Crédit Agricole**

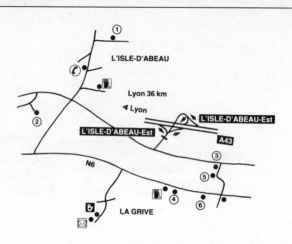

Hotels
1. **Relais du Catey** L L'Isle-d'Abeau, 38300 Bourgoin-Jallieu ☎ 74 27 02 97 F:8
2. **Campanile** L L'Isle-d-Abeau, 38300 Bourgoin-Jallieu ☎ 74 27 01 22
3. **Climat de France** L L'Isle-d'Abeau, 38300 Bourgoin-Jallieu ☎ 74 28 52 29

Rests 4. **Petite Aub.** (*avec ch*) L La Grive, 38300 Bourgoin-Jallieu ☎ 74 93 48 52 F:8,S
Garages 5. **BMA** (Citroën)
S/marché 6. **Intermarché**

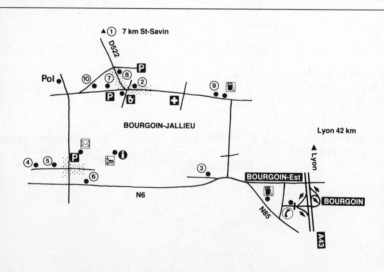

Hotels
1. **La Rivière** L St-Savin, 38300 Bourgoin-Jallieu ☎ 74 93 72 16 F:8,D(s),Me
2. **Commerce** L av. Tixier, 38300 Bourgoin-Jallieu ☎ 74 93 38 01 F:8,D

Garages 3. **Parenton** (Ford) 4. **Pellet** (Citroën) 5. **Pin** (Renault)
Banques 6. **Crédit Agricole** 7. **Banque Laydernier** 8. **Crédit Agricole** 9. **Caisse d'Epargne**
S/marché 10. **Genty**

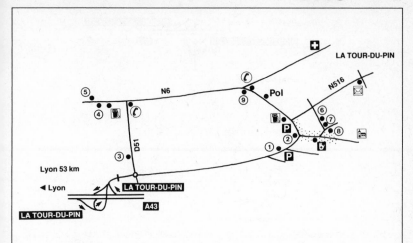

Hotels ① **France** L 38110 La Tour-du-Pin ☎ 74 97 00 08
② **Dauphiné Savoie** L 38110 La Tour-du-Pin ☎ 74 97 03 87 F:3,10,L(m)
Garages ③ **Ferraz** (Volvo) ④ **Tour-Autos** (Renault) ⑤ **Vial** (Citroën)
Banques ⑥ **Caisse d'Epargne** ⑦ **Banque Populaire** ⑧ **BNP**
S/marché ⑨ **Genty**

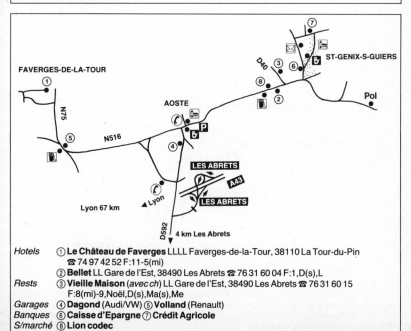

Hotels ① **Le Château de Faverges** LLLL Faverges-de-la-Tour, 38110 La Tour-du-Pin
☎ 74 97 42 52 F:11-5(mi)
② **Bellet** LL Gare de l'Est, 38490 Les Abrets ☎ 76 31 60 04 F:1,D(s),L
Rests ③ **Vieille Maison** (*avec ch*) LL Gare de l'Est, 38490 Les Abrets ☎ 76 31 60 15
F:8(mi)-9,Noël,D(s),Ma(s),Me
Garages ④ **Dagond** (Audi/VW) ⑤ **Volland** (Renault)
Banques ⑥ **Caisse d'Epargne** ⑦ **Crédit Agricole**
S/marché ⑧ **Lion codec**

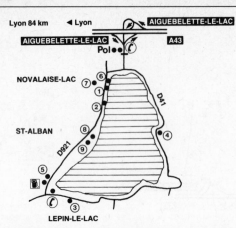

Hotels	① **Novalaise-Plage** LL 73470 Novalaise ☎ 79 36 02 19 F:11-3,L(s),Ma	
	② **St-Alban-Plage** (*sans rest*) LL 73610 Lépin-le-Lac ☎ 79 36 02 05 F:11-4	
	③ **Clos Savoyard** L 73610 Lépin-le-Lac ☎ 79 36 00 15 F:9(mi)-5	
Rests	④ **Chez Michelon** (*avec ch*) L 73610 Lépin ☎ 79 36 05 02 F:10,11,Noël,L(s),Ma	
Garages	⑤ **Villeton** (Renault)	
Camping	⑥ **L'Ambroisière** 73470 Novalaise ☎ 79 36 04 76 F:11-3	
	⑦ **Les Charmilles** 73470 Novalaise ☎ 79 36 04 67 F:9-6	
	⑧ **Base de Loisirs du Sougey** St-Alban, 73610 Lépin ☎ 79 36 01 44 F:11-3	
	⑨ **Bellevue** St-Alban, 73610 Lépin-le-Lac ☎ 79 36 01 48 F:11-4	

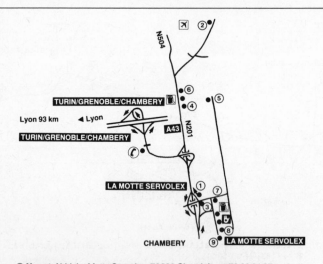

Hotels	① **Novotel** LLL La Motte Servolex, 73000 Chambéry ☎79 69 21 27	
	② **Cerf Volant** LLL Voglans, 73420 Viviers-du-Lac ☎ 79 54 40 44 F:Noël	
	③ **Ibis** L La Motte Servolex, 73000 Chambéry ☎ 79 69 28 36	
Garages	④ **Lain** (Audi/VW) ⑤ **Dieu** (Citroën) ⑥ **Comtet** (Peugeot-Talbot)	
	⑦ **Chambéry Nord Auto** (Renault)	
S/marché	⑧ **Chamnord** ⑨ **Carrefour**	

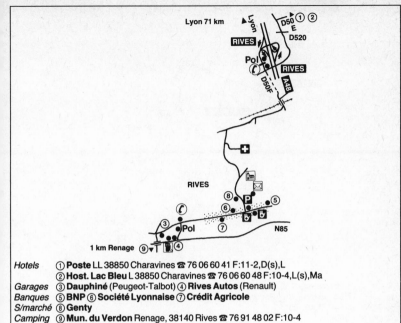

Hotels
① **Poste** LL 38850 Charavines ☎ 76 06 60 41 F:11-2,D(s),L
② **Host. Lac Bleu** L 38850 Charavines ☎ 76 06 60 48 F:10-4,L(s),Ma
Garages ③ **Dauphiné** (Peugeot-Talbot) ④ **Rives Autos** (Renault)
Banques ⑤ **BNP** ⑥ **Société Lyonnaise** ⑦ **Crédit Agricole**
S/marché ⑧ **Genty**
Camping ⑨ **Mun. du Verdon** Renage, 38140 Rives ☎ 76 91 48 02 F:10-4

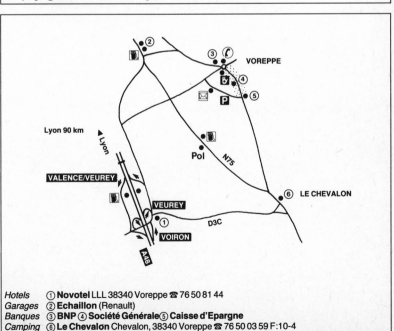

Hotels ① **Novotel** LLL 38340 Voreppe ☎ 76 50 81 44
Garages ② **Echaillon** (Renault)
Banques ③ **BNP** ④ **Société Générale** ⑤ **Caisse d'Epargne**
Camping ⑥ **Le Chevalon** Chevalon, 38340 Voreppe ☎ 76 50 03 59 F:10-4

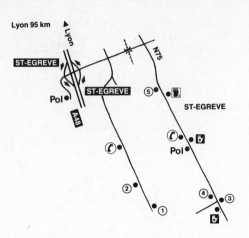

Hotels ① **Campanile** L 38120 St-Egrève ☎ 76 75 57 88
Garages ② **St-Egrève Auto** (Peugeot-Talbot) ③ **Guillaumin** (Audi/VW)
Banques ④ **Crédit Agricole**
S/marché ⑤ **Genty**

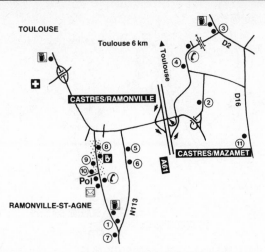

Hotels ① **La Chaumière** LLL 31520 Ramonville-St-Agne ☎ 61 73 02 02
② **Ariane** LL 31400 Toulouse ☎ 61 34 06 05
Garages ③ **Autos Services** (Ford) ④ **Ichard** (Renault) ⑤ **Succursale** (Citroën) ⑥ **Renault**
⑦ **S.I.A.L.** (Peugeot-Talbot)
Banques ⑧ **Caisse d'Epargne** ⑨ **Crédit Agricole** ⑩ **Société Générale**
S/marché ⑪ **Carrefour**

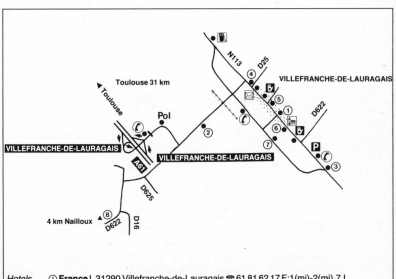

Hotels ① **France** L 31290 Villefranche-de-Lauragais ☎ 61 81 62 17 F:1(mi)-2(mi),7,L
Garages ② **Fontez** (Renault) ③ **Granier** (Ford) ④ **Moderne** (Peugeot-Talbot)
Banques ⑤ **Crédit Agricole** ⑥ **Caisse d'Epargne**
S/marché ⑦ **Lauragais**
Camping ⑧ **Le Parc de la Thésauque** 31560 Nailloux ☎ 61 81 34 67

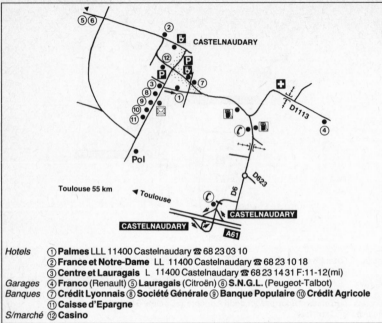

Hotels
① **Palmes** LLL 11400 Castelnaudary ☎ 68 23 03 10
② **France et Notre-Dame** LL 11400 Castelnaudary ☎ 68 23 10 18
③ **Centre et Lauragais** L 11400 Castelnaudary ☎ 68 23 14 31 F:11-12(mi)
Garages ④ **Franco** (Renault) ⑤ **Lauragais** (Citroën) ⑥ **S.N.G.L.** (Peugeot-Talbot)
Banques ⑦ **Crédit Lyonnais** ⑧ **Société Générale** ⑨ **Banque Populaire** ⑩ **Crédit Agricole**
⑪ **Caisse d'Epargne**
S/marché ⑫ **Casino**

Hotels
① **Domaine d'Auriac** LLL 11000 Carcassonne ☎ 68 25 72 22 F:1,D,L(mi)
② **Motel Salvaza** LL 11000 Carcassonne ☎ 68 25 02 73
③ **Montségur** LL 11000 Carcassonne ☎ 68 25 31 41
Garages ④ **Ménard** (Citroën) ⑤ **Audoise** (Peugeot-Talbot) ⑥ **Vigual** (Fiat) ⑦ **Laporta** (Ford)
Banques ⑧ **Banque Populaire** ⑨ **Société Générale** ⑩ **Crédit Agricole** ⑪ **BNP**
S/marché ⑫ **Mammouth** ⑬ **Leclerc**
Camping ⑭ **Les Lavandières** Pennautier, 11000 Carcassonne ☎ 68 25 41 66 F:10-5

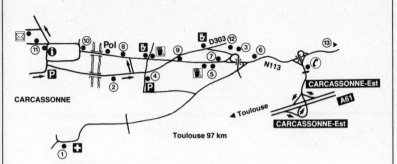

Hotels		
	① **Domaine d'Auriac** LLL 11000 Carcassonne ☎ 68 25 72 22 F:1,D,L(mi)	
	② **Pont Vieux** (*sans rest*) LL 11000 Carcassonne ☎ 68 25 24 99 F:1	
	③ **Ibis** L 11000 Carcassonne ☎ 68 47 98 35	
	④ **Aragon** (*sans rest*) L 11000 Carcassonne ☎ 68 47 16 31	
	⑤ **Climat de France** L 11000 Carcassonne ☎ 68 71 16 20	
Garages	⑥ **Cathala** (Audi/VW) ⑦ **Alaux et Gestin** (Renault) ⑧ **Claret** (BMW)	
Banques	⑨ **Crédit Agricole** ⑩ **Crédit Lyonnais** ⑪ **Banque Populaire**	
S/marché	⑫ **Euromarché**	
Camping	⑬ **Municipal** 11800 Trèbes ☎ 68 78 61 75 F:9(mi)-6(mi)	

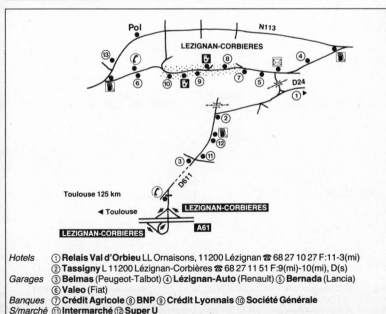

Hotels		
	① **Relais Val d'Orbieu** LL Ornaisons, 11200 Lézignan ☎ 68 27 10 27 F:11-3(mi)	
	② **Tassigny** L 11200 Lézignan-Corbières ☎ 68 27 11 51 F:9(mi)-10(mi), D(s)	
Garages	③ **Belmas** (Peugeot-Talbot) ④ **Lézignan-Auto** (Renault) ⑤ **Bernada** (Lancia)	
	⑥ **Valeo** (Fiat)	
Banques	⑦ **Crédit Agricole** ⑧ **BNP** ⑨ **Crédit Lyonnais** ⑩ **Société Générale**	
S/marché	⑪ **Intermarché** ⑫ **Super U**	
Camping	⑬ **Mun. la Pinède** 11200 Lézignan-Corbières ☎ 68 27 05 08 F:12-2	

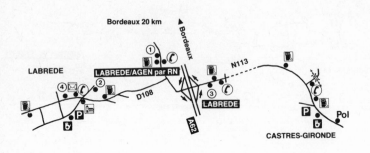

Garages ① **La Prade** (Audi/VW) ② **Bellon** (Renault) ③ **Danglade** (Peugeot-Talbot)
Banques ④ **Caisse d'Epargne**

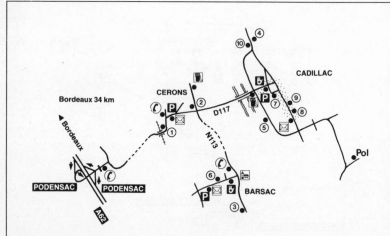

Hotels   ① **Grappe d'Or** L Cérons, 33720 Podensac ☎ 56 27 11 61 F:1
        ② **Grillobois** L Cérons, 33720 Podensac ☎ 56 27 11 50 F:8,Noël,S,D
Rests   ③ **Château de Rolland** (*avec ch*) LLL Barsac, 33720 Podensac ☎ 56 27 15 75 F:11
Garages ④ **Foucal** (Renault) ⑤ **Ducos** (Audi/VW)
Banques ⑥ **Caisse d'Epargne** ⑦ **BNP** ⑧ **Crédit Lyonnais** ⑨ **Caisse d'Epargne**
S/marché ⑩ **Maxicoop**

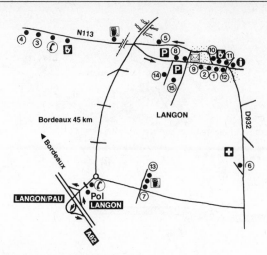

Hotels ① **Modern** L 33210 Langon ☎ 56 63 06 65
Rests ② **Claude Darroze** (*avec ch*) LL 33210 Langon ☎ 56 63 00 48 F:10-11(mi),D(s),L
Garages ③ **Messines** (Renault) ④ **Saga** (Citroën) ⑤ **SO.GI.DA** (Mercedes) ⑥ **Cransac** (Audi/VW)
⑦ **Doux et Trouillot** (Peugeot-Talbot)
Banques ⑧ **Créd. Agricole** ⑨ **Soc. Gén.** ⑩ **Crédit Lyonnais** ⑪ **Banque Pop.** ⑫ **BNP**
S/marché ⑬ **Intermarché** ⑭ **Leclerc** ⑮ **Sodiprix**

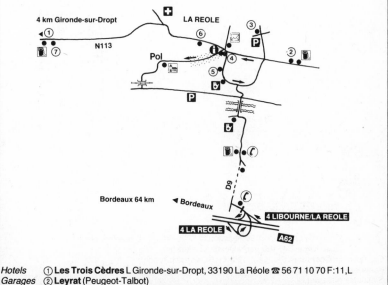

Hotels ① **Les Trois Cèdres** L Gironde-sur-Dropt, 33190 La Réole ☎ 56 71 10 70 F:11,L
Garages ② **Leyrat** (Peugeot-Talbot)
Banques ③ **Crédit Agricole** ④ **Société Générale** ⑤ **BNP** ⑥ **Caisse d'Epargne**
S/marché ⑦ **Intermarché**

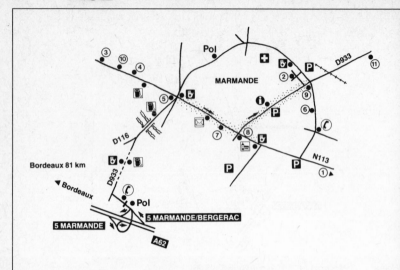

Hotels ① **Capricorne** LL 47200 Marmande ☎ 53 64 16 14
② **Aub. de Guyenne** L 47200 Marmande ☎ 53 64 01 77 F:11-2
Garages ③ **Auto-Aquitaine** (Ford) ④ **Mayet** (Peugeot-Talbot) ⑤ **Deldon** (Renault) ⑥ **Lamat** (Opel)
Banques ⑦ **Crédit Agricole** ⑧ **Société Générale** ⑨ **Banque Populaire**
S/marché ⑩ **Suma** ⑪ **Mammouth**

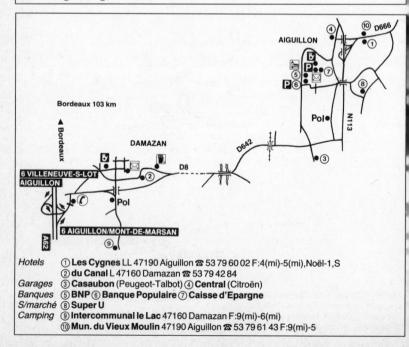

Hotels ① **Les Cygnes** LL 47190 Aiguillon ☎ 53 79 60 02 F:4(mi)-5(mi),Noël-1,S
② **du Canal** L 47160 Damazan ☎ 53 79 42 84
Garages ③ **Casaubon** (Peugeot-Talbot) ④ **Central** (Citroën)
Banques ⑤ **BNP** ⑥ **Banque Populaire** ⑦ **Caisse d'Epargne**
S/marché ⑧ **Super U**
Camping ⑨ **Intercommunal le Lac** 47160 Damazan F:9(mi)-6(mi)
⑩ **Mun. du Vieux Moulin** 47190 Aiguillon ☎ 53 79 61 43 F:9(mi)-5

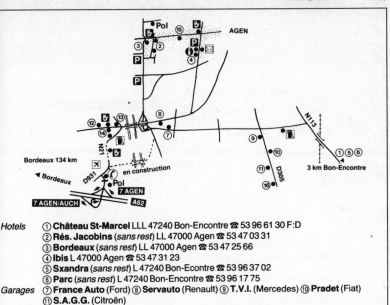

Hotels
① **Château St-Marcel** LLL 47240 Bon-Encontre ☎ 53 96 61 30 F:D
② **Rés. Jacobins** (*sans rest*) LL 47000 Agen ☎ 53 47 03 31
③ **Bordeaux** (*sans rest*) LL 47000 Agen ☎ 53 47 25 66
④ **Ibis** L 47000 Agen ☎ 53 47 31 23
⑤ **Sxandra** (*sans rest*) L 47240 Bon-Encontre ☎ 53 96 37 02
⑥ **Parc** (*sans rest*) L 47240 Bon-Encontre ☎ 53 96 17 75
Garages ⑦ **France Auto** (Ford) ⑧ **Servauto** (Renault) ⑨ **T.V.I.** (Mercedes) ⑩ **Pradet** (Fiat)
⑪ **S.A.G.G.** (Citroën)
Banques ⑫ **BNP** ⑬ **Crédit Agricole** ⑭ **Banque Populaire** ⑮ **Crédit Lyonnais**
S/marché ⑯ **Mammouth**

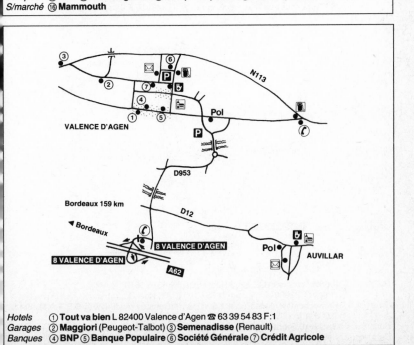

Hotels ① **Tout va bien** L 82400 Valence d'Agen ☎ 63 39 54 83 F:1
Garages ② **Maggiori** (Peugeot-Talbot) ③ **Semenadisse** (Renault)
Banques ④ **BNP** ⑤ **Banque Populaire** ⑥ **Société Générale** ⑦ **Crédit Agricole**

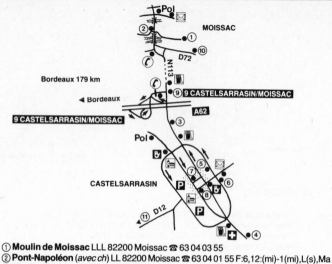

Hotels   ① **Moulin de Moissac** LLL 82200 Moissac ☎ 63 04 03 55
Rests   ② **Pont-Napoléon** (*avec ch*) LL 82200 Moissac ☎ 63 04 01 55 F:6,12:(mi)-1(mi),L(s),Ma
Garages   ③ **Martin** (Citroën) ④ **Dupart** (Renault)
Banques   ⑤ **Caisse d'Epargne** ⑥ **Société Générale** ⑦ **BNP** ⑧ **Banque Populaire**
S/marché ⑨ **Intermarché**
Camping   ⑩ **Mun. l'Ile de Bidounet** 82200 Moissac ☎ 63 32 29 96 F:10-3
          ⑪ **S.I Trescasses** 82100 Castelsarrasin ☎ 63 32 30 37 F:9(mi)-6(mi)

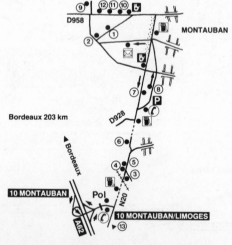

Hotels   ① **Ingres** (*sans rest*) LLL 82000 Montauban ☎ 63 63 36 01
          ② **Orsay** LL 82000 Montauban ☎ 63 63 00 57 F:5,Noël,D,L(m)
Garages   ③ **Hamecher** (Mercedes) ④ **M.A.S.** (Opel) ⑤ **Delpoux** (Audi/VW) ⑥ **S.E.T.A.M.** (Ford)
          ⑦ **S.O.D.A.M.** (Fiat) ⑧ **Gardette** (Lancia) ⑨ **Macard** (Peugeot-Talbot)
Banques   ⑩ **Société Générale** ⑪ **Banque Populaire** ⑫ **Crédit Agricole**
Camping   ⑬ **Fongrave** Montbartier, 82700 Montech ☎ 63 30 52 73 F:9(mi)-5

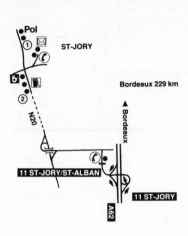

Garages ① **Platanes** (Renault) ② **Anon** (Peugeot-Talbot)

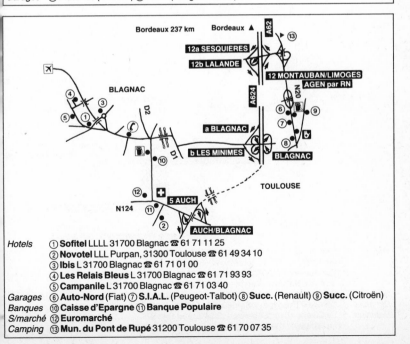

Hotels
① **Sofitel** LLLL 31700 Blagnac ☎ 61 71 11 25
② **Novotel** LLL Purpan, 31300 Toulouse ☎ 61 49 34 10
③ **Ibis** L 31700 Blagnac ☎ 61 71 01 00
④ **Les Relais Bleus** L 31700 Blagnac ☎ 61 71 93 93
⑤ **Campanile** L 31700 Blagnac ☎ 61 71 03 40
Garages ⑥ **Auto-Nord** (Fiat) ⑦ **S.I.A.L.** (Peugeot-Talbot) ⑧ **Succ.** (Renault) ⑨ **Succ.** (Citroën)
Banques ⑩ **Caisse d'Epargne** ⑪ **Banque Populaire**
S/marché ⑫ **Euromarché**
Camping ⑬ **Mun. du Pont de Rupé** 31200 Toulouse ☎ 61 70 07 35

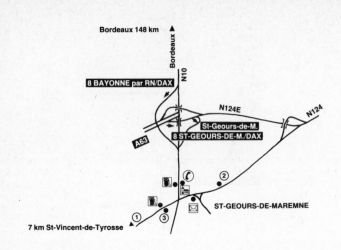

Hotels ① **Twickenham** L 40230 St-Vincent-de-Tyrosse ☎ 58 77 01 60 F:9(mi)-10(mi),L
Garages ② **Anon** (Peugeot-Talbot)
Banques ③ **Crédit Agricole**

Hotels ① **Océan** LL 40130 Capbreton ☎ 58 72 10 22 F:11-2
       ② **Miramar** LL 40130 Capbreton ☎ 58 72 12 82 F:9(mi)-4
       ③ **Terrasses** L 40130 Capbreton ☎ 58 72 10 20 F:10(mi)-5(mi)
       ④ **Centre** L Benesse-Maremne, 40230 St-Vincent ☎ 58 77 04 16 F:11,L
Garages ⑤ **Barbe** (Citroën) ⑥ **Atlantic** (Renault) ⑦ **Autocap** (Audi/VW)
Banques ⑧ **Caisse d'Epargne** ⑨ **Société Générale** ⑩ **BNP** ⑪ **Crédit Lyonnais**
Camping ⑫ **La Civelle** 40130 Capbreton ☎ 58 72 15 11 F:10-5
       ⑬ **La Pointe** 40130 Capbreton ☎ 58 72 14 98 F:9(mi)-6(mi)

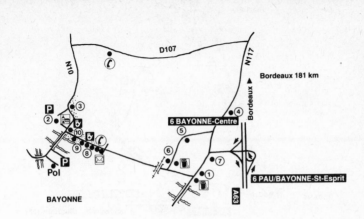

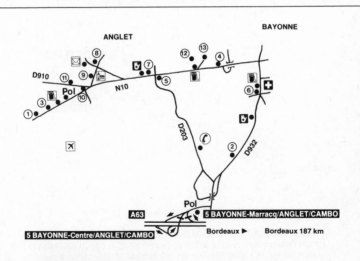

Hotels   ① **Aria** LL 64100 Bayonne ☎ 59 55 22 70
② **Loustau** LL 64100 Bayonne ☎ 59 55 16 74 F:12(mi)-1
③ **Côte Basque** (*sans rest*) L 64100 Bayonne ☎ 59 55 10 21
Garages   ④ **Descoubes** (Saab) ⑤ **Marmande** (Austin-Rover) ⑥ **Auto Bayonne** (Toyota)
⑦ **Vara** (Audi/VW)
Banques   ⑧ **Société Générale** ⑨ **Caisse d'Epargne** ⑩ **BNP**

Hotels   ① **Ibis** L 64600 Anglet ☎ 59 03 45 45
② **Mendi Alde** (*sans rest*) L 64100 Bayonne ☎ 59 63 58 44
Garages   ③ **Aylies** (Renault) ④ **Gambade** (Peugeot-Talbot) ⑤ **Côte Basque** (Citroën)
Banques   ⑥ **Société Générale** ⑦ **Banque Populaire** ⑧ **Crédit Agricole** ⑨ **Caisse d'Epargne**
⑩ **BNP** ⑪ **Crédit Lyonnais**
S/marché   ⑫ **Géant Casino** ⑬ **Carrefour**

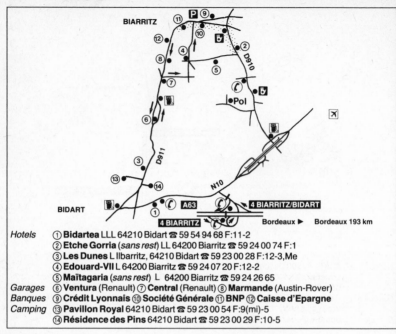

Hotels
① **Bidartea** LLL 64210 Bidart ☎ 59 54 94 68 F:11-2
② **Etche Gorria** (*sans rest*) LL 64200 Biarritz ☎ 59 24 00 74 F:1
③ **Les Dunes** L Ilbarritz, 64210 Bidart ☎ 59 23 00 28 F:12-3,Me
④ **Edouard-VII** L 64200 Biarritz ☎ 59 24 07 20 F:12-2
⑤ **Maïtagaria** (*sans rest*) L 64200 Biarritz ☎ 59 24 26 65
Garages ⑥ **Ventura** (Renault) ⑦ **Central** (Renault) ⑧ **Marmande** (Austin-Rover)
Banques ⑨ **Crédit Lyonnais** ⑩ **Société Générale** ⑪ **BNP** ⑫ **Caisse d'Epargne**
Camping ⑬ **Pavillon Royal** 64210 Bidart ☎ 59 23 00 54 F:9(mi)-5
⑭ **Résidence des Pins** 64210 Bidart ☎ 59 23 00 29 F:10-5

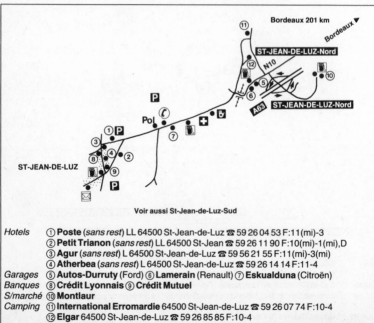

Hotels
① **Poste** (*sans rest*) LL 64500 St-Jean-de-Luz ☎ 59 26 04 53 F:11(mi)-3
② **Petit Trianon** (*sans rest*) LL 64500 St-Jean ☎ 59 26 11 90 F:10(mi)-1(mi),D
③ **Agur** (*sans rest*) L 64500 St-Jean-de-Luz ☎ 59 56 21 55 F:11(mi)-3(mi)
④ **Atherbea** (*sans rest*) L 64500 St-Jean-de-Luz ☎ 59 26 14 14 F:11-4
Garages ⑤ **Autos-Durruty** (Ford) ⑥ **Lamerain** (Renault) ⑦ **Eskualduna** (Citroën)
Banques ⑧ **Crédit Lyonnais** ⑨ **Crédit Mutuel**
S/marché ⑩ **Montlaur**
Camping ⑪ **International Erromardie** 64500 St-Jean-de-Luz ☎ 59 26 07 74 F:10-4
⑫ **Elgar** 64500 St-Jean-de-Luz ☎ 59 26 85 85 F:10-4

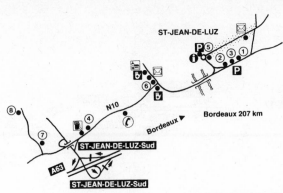

Hotels	① **Commerce** (*sans rest*) LL 64500 St-Jean-de-Luz ☎ 59 26 31 99
	② **Continental** L 64500 St-Jean-de-Luz ☎ 59 26 01 23 F:11
	③ **Paris** (*sans rest*) L 64500 St-Jean-de-Luz ☎ 59 26 00 62 F:12(mi)-2(mi)
Garages	④ **SAKA** (Peugeot-Talbot) ⑤ **Lamerain** (Renault)
Banques	⑥ **BNP**
Camping	⑦ **Larrouleta** 64122 Urrugne ☎ 59 47 37 84
	⑧ **Suhiberry** 64122 Urrugne ☎ 59 47 06 23 F:9(mi)-5

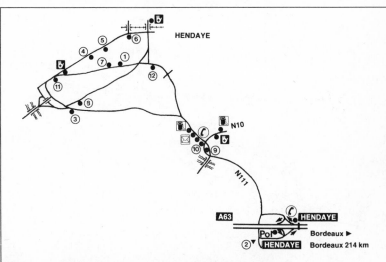

Hotels	① **Sud-Américain** L 64700 Hendaye ☎ 59 20 75 98 F:10-5
Rests	② **Bakéa** (*avec ch*) LL Biriatou, 64700 Hendaye ☎ 59 20 76 36 F:10-5(mi)
Garages	③ **Pivot** (Opel) ④ **International** (Fiat) ⑤ **Hendaye-Autos** (Renault)
	⑥ **Laguillon** (Peugeot-Talbot) ⑦ **Xaby** (Ford) ⑧ **de la Place** (Citroën)
Banques	⑨ **Banque Inchauspe** ⑩ **Banque Populaire** ⑪ **Banco de Bilbao**
S/marché	⑫ **Champion**

A72/A47

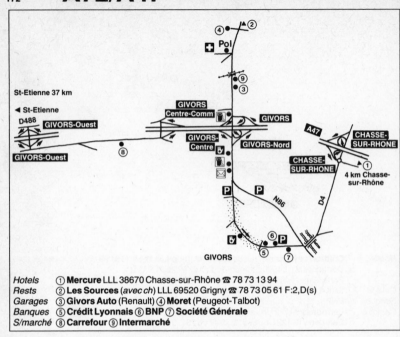

Hotels	① **Mercure** LLL 38670 Chasse-sur-Rhône ☎ 78 73 13 94
Rests	② **Les Sources** (*avec ch*) LLL 69520 Grigny ☎ 78 73 05 61 F:2,D(s)
Garages	③ **Givors Auto** (Renault) ④ **Moret** (Peugeot-Talbot)
Banques	⑤ **Crédit Lyonnais** ⑥ **BNP** ⑦ **Société Générale**
S/marché	⑧ **Carrefour** ⑨ **Intermarché**

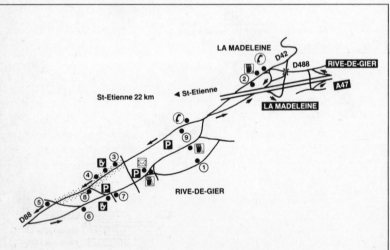

Rests	① **Host. Renaissance** (*avec ch*) LLL 42800 Rive-de-Gier ☎ 77 75 04 31
Garages	② **Merle** (Audi/VW)
Banques	③ **Crédit Agricole** ④ **Banque Populaire** ⑤ **BNP** ⑥ **Crédit Lyonnais**
	⑦ **Caisse d'Epargne** ⑧ **Société Générale**
S/marché	⑨ **Intermarché**

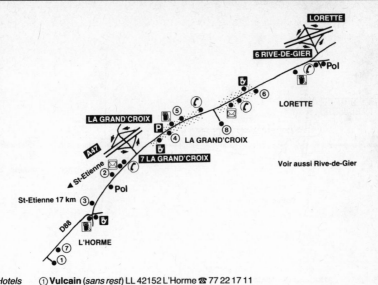

Hotels   ① **Vulcain** (*sans rest*) LL 42152 L'Horme ☎ 77 22 17 11
Garages   ② **Chambon** (Renault) ③ **Bachasse** (Citroën)
Banques   ④ **Crédit Agricole** ⑤ **Caisse d'Epargne** ⑥ **Crédit Agricole**
S/marché   ⑦ **Intermarché** ⑧ **Europrix**

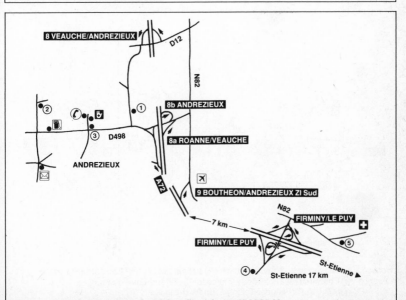

Hotels   ① **Novotel** LLL 42160 Andrézieux-Bouthéon ☎ 77 36 55 63
Garages   ② **G.A.M.M.A.** (Austin-Rover)
S/marché   ③ **Suma** ④ **Rond point** ⑤ **Casino**

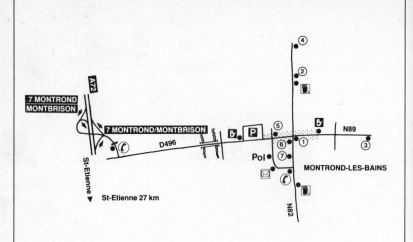

Hotels ① **Host. La Poularde** LLL 42210 Montrond-les-Bains ☎ 77 54 40 06 F:1,L(s),Ma(m)
② **Motel du Forez** (*sans rest*) L 42210 Montrond-les-Bains ☎ 77 54 42 28
Garages ③ **Décultieux** (Renault) ④ **Protière** (Citroën)
Banques ⑤ **Crédit Lyonnais** ⑥ **Caisse d'Epargne** ⑦ **Banque Populaire**

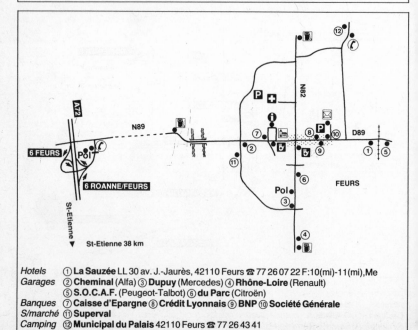

Hotels ① **La Sauzée** LL 30 av. J.-Jaurès, 42110 Feurs ☎ 77 26 07 22 F:10(mi)-11(mi),Me
Garages ② **Cheminal** (Alfa) ③ **Dupuy** (Mercedes) ④ **Rhône-Loire** (Renault)
⑤ **S.O.C.A.F.** (Peugeot-Talbot) ⑥ **du Parc** (Citroën)
Banques ⑦ **Caisse d'Epargne** ⑧ **Crédit Lyonnais** ⑨ **BNP** ⑩ **Société Générale**
S/marché ⑪ **Superval**
Camping ⑫ **Municipal du Palais** 42110 Feurs ☎ 77 26 43 41

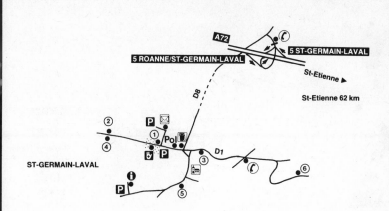

Hotels ① **Aub. des Voyageurs** L 42260 St-Germain-Laval ☎ 77 65 40 84 F:2,11,D(s),L
② **Touristes** L 42260 St-Germain-Laval ☎ 77 65 41 08 F:2,Ma(9-6)
Garages ③ **Rambaud** (Peugeot-Talbot)
Banques ④ **Crédit Agricole** ⑤ **Caisse d'Epargne**
Camping ⑥ **Municipal la Pras** 42260 St-Germain-Laval ☎ 77 65 44 35 F:10-3

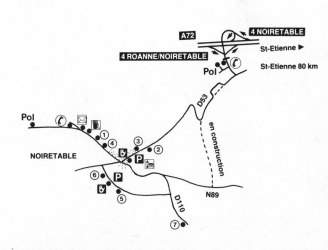

Hotels ① **La Chaumière** LL 42440 Noirétable ☎ 77 24 73 00 F:11-2
Garages ② **Dejob** (Renault)
Banques ③ **Caisse d'Epargne** ④ **Crédit Lyonnais** ⑤ **Crédit Agricole**
S/marché ⑥ **Toun-ky**
Camping ⑦ **Municipal de la Roche** 42440 Noirétable ☎ 77 24 72 68 F:11-3

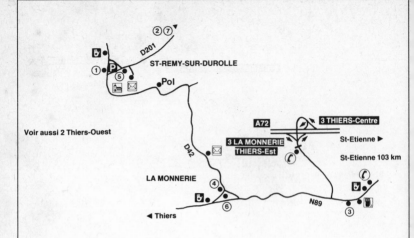

Hotels	① **Voyageurs** L 63550 St-Rémy-sur-Durolle ☎ 73 94 30 53 F:12
Rests	② **Vieux Logis** (*avec ch*) L 63550 St-Rémy-sur-Durolle ☎ 73 94 30 78 F:2,9,D(s),L
Garages	③ **Robledo** (Ford)
Banques	④ **Crédit Agricole** ⑤ **Crédit Agricole**
S/marché	⑥ **Suma**
Camping	⑦ **Mun. les Chanterelles** 63550 St-Rémy-sur-Durolle ☎ 73 94 31 71 F:10-4

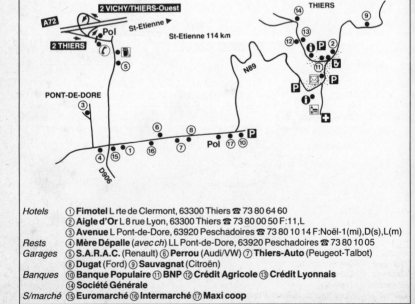

Hotels	① **Fimotel** L rte de Clermont, 63300 Thiers ☎ 73 80 64 60
	② **Aigle d'Or** L 8 rue Lyon, 63300 Thiers ☎ 73 80 00 50 F:11,L
	③ **Avenue** L Pont-de-Dore, 63920 Peschadoires ☎ 73 80 10 14 F:Noël-1(mi),D(s),L(m)
Rests	④ **Mère Dépalle** (*avec ch*) LL Pont-de-Dore, 63920 Peschadoires ☎ 73 80 10 05
Garages	⑤ **S.A.R.A.C.** (Renault) ⑥ **Perrou** (Audi/VW) ⑦ **Thiers-Auto** (Peugeot-Talbot)
	⑧ **Dugat** (Ford) ⑨ **Sauvagnat** (Citroën)
Banques	⑩ **Banque Populaire** ⑪ **BNP** ⑫ **Crédit Agricole** ⑬ **Crédit Lyonnais**
	⑭ **Société Générale**
S/marché	⑮ **Euromarché** ⑯ **Intermarché** ⑰ **Maxi coop**